BARRON'S PARE

KEYS TO
RAISING A
DEAF CHILD

Virginia Frazier-Maiwald

Lenore M. Williams, M.A.

DOUGHERTY
COUNTY
PUBLIC
LIBRARY

BARRON'S

Cover Photo and text photography by James McDonald, educator and photographer, Gilroy, California

DEDICATION
For my loving husband, Kevin Maiwald, and my children, Meghan and Sean. In memory of my father, John Robert Frazier, who would have been proud of this work and even more proud of his grandchildren, who were the inspiration for this book.

To my husband, John Williams, who has been by my side through all of life's challenges, and to my two lovely daughters, Katie and Maggie. In loving memory of my aunt, Agnes Healy, who would have enjoyed the publication of this book.

All inquiries should be addressed to:
Barron's Educational Series, Inc.
250 Wireless Boulevard
Hauppauge, New York 11788
http://www.barronseduc.com

Library of Congress Catalog Card No. 98-50393

International Standard Book No. 0-7641-0723-2

Library of Congress Cataloging-in-Publication Data
Frazier-Maiwald, Virginia.
    Keys to raising a deaf child / Virginia Frazier-Maiwald, Lenore M. Williams.
        p.   cm. — (Barron's parenting keys)
    Includes bibliographical references (p.   ) and index.
    ISBN 0-7641-0723-2
    1. Deaf children—Language. 2. Deaf children—Education. 3. Deaf children—Family relationships. I. Williams, Lenore M. II. Title. III. Series.
HV2391.F7   1999
649'.1512—dc21   98-50393
                                                                        CIP

PRINTED IN THE UNITED STATES OF AMERICA
987654321

CONTENTS

INTRODUCTION

L anguage learning is a natural process. Hearing children acquire language from listening and interacting with their environment. Language learning in deaf and hard-of-hearing children is not always as spontaneous and easy. However, many deaf or hard-of-hearing children acquire language quickly, naturally, and comprehensively. The foundation for language learning begins with a strong parent-child bond and an environment that supports a deaf child's special needs. This book provides parents with information, tips, and suggestions for fostering a nurturing and language-rich environment for a deaf or hard-of-hearing child.

Throughout this book, the term deaf is used inclusively. In most cases the information, tips, and suggestions are appropriate for hard-of-hearing as well as deaf children. The ability to hear and decipher speech is a complicated process. Each child's hearing loss, ability to use amplification, and inherent ability to acquire language is different. Furthermore, some children's hearing losses change over time, sometimes becoming more severe.

Our perspective is to nurture the whole child. Value your child's unique attributes. Reinforce his or her strengths in whatever area they may lie. Strive to expose your child to enriching experiences in the home, school, and community. There is no one as qualified as yourself to support and love your child. Take the time to communicate with your child. Enjoy your child as an individual. Developing your child's self-esteem is one of the greatest gifts you can give him or her.

ACKNOWLEDGMENTS

We would like to acknowledge the following people for their contributions and support: Manny Barbara, Terry Crump, Karen Denman, Evette Dilley, Virginia Frazier, the Frazier family, Susan Ganske, Gerilee Gustason, the Healy family, Kathleen Healy, Barbara Leutke-Stahlman, the Maiwald family, Ellen Mastman, Adeline McClatchie, James McDonald, Paul Ogden, the Oswald family, Adrienne Renner, Maggie Rollings, James Russell, Maria Trevino, Linda Turner, Elizabeth Watson-Semmons, and Marjorie Williams.

1

~~~~~~

AFFIRMING YOUR CHILD'S HEARING LOSS

Accepting my daughter's deafness was not difficult for me. For months, I knew something in her development was not normal. At times, I believed her to be deaf yet then she would react to a particular sound or say a simple word such as "up" or "Papa" and the cycle of confusion would continue. Other possibilities crossed my mind and worried me more than deafness. It was a relief that she was finally diagnosed at two years old as having a severe to profound sensorineural hearing loss.

My training and experience as a bilingual educator played an important role in coping with the issues and decisions revolving around deafness. I knew the task before us was enormous. More important, I also knew that our family needed to develop a communication system that was inclusive of Meghan. Once given enough understandable communication in an appropriate mode, Meghan would have the potential to learn and grow cognitively just as any other child.

Certainly communication was of utmost importance, and for this reason, our first task was to become proficient in sign language quickly. I knew that it was imperative to her success that we become communication role models.

Schools cannot accomplish this alone. We enjoyed becoming a bimodal family, using signs to match our spoken words. At times, the commitment to classes and practicing was difficult. I look back on those early years as money in the bank. It seemed that so much time and effort went into communicating with our daughter and we just weren't being paid off with fluency in conversations. Now, four years later, the dividends are multiplying. Meghan is mainstreamed, has good self-esteem, and enjoys playmates who are deaf and hearing.

It was with surprising shock that I reacted to the news that our second child, a son, was also born deaf. I remember feeling overwhelmed, but mostly tired. For many hearing parents, deaf children require more work, energy, time, and patience. This time, it was our experience with Meghan that helped us cope. Her attitude buoyed us. Meghan was thrilled! Sean would soon have hearing aids just like she had. The dividends of early signing paid off much sooner the second time around. Sean signed his first perfect sign at eight months. He reached two milestones simultaneously as he pulled his little body up to a stance next to the coffee table and signed, "Hello!"

My experiences have taught me that expedient parental action is essential. I felt pushy as I repeatedly told my daughter's pediatrician that something was not normal. Now, I wish I had been more persistent.

Intensive and early intervention may result in early communication competencies. This applies to testing and evaluations, hearing aids, school placement, and therapy. It is important to follow through on all appointments and secure the information to take the next step. Develop a system to track all the information. A binder or files will be helpful to keep the information organized and easily accessible.

You will need to be persistent. Working through the myriad of information, decisions, and choices thrust upon you may become overwhelming. Immediately following your child's diagnosis, contact your local school district to have your child evaluated and to become informed of available programs. Such programs and procedures will vary in different areas. As a parent of a child with special needs, you have rights. Get involved in your child's education and network with other parents. Don't wait! Each day your child is without service is another day of missed language opportunities.

Find support wherever you can: family, friends, other parents of deaf children, or the Deaf community. You will also need someone to be there for you emotionally, mentally, and physically. If your spouse is in denial or is grieving, find someone who can be there for you. However, be accepting of your spouse. Each person grieves in his or her own way. Some people take a long time to absorb and cope with new realities. Eventually, your spouse may become an advocate for your child and a tremendous support for you. Continue to move forward, even if you feel your spouse is not moving quickly enough through the grieving process.

Get a trusted family member or friend to care for your child occasionally. You will need breaks. Working with your child will become exhausting and frustrating at times. Bring someone to every appointment. The information may get overwhelming and your support person may retain essential information you do not.

I remember talking to a parent whose child's hearing loss was caused by a drug the child was given in the hospital. The mother was upset because the doctor never told her that giving this drug could cause a hearing loss. The child's grandfather happened to be at home that day. He remembered hearing the doctor tell the mother that a hearing loss was a possible side effect of using the drug. The mother was so upset that she only focused on saving her daughter's life and didn't even hear the side effects of the medicine. This is an emotional time for parents. Anything that hurts your child deeply wounds you, the parent. An advocate can help you keep track of the information overload.

2

COPING STRATEGIES

This is a stressful time for any couple. Remember that blame and recriminations are counterproductive. You must start today with a new reality and figure out how you are going to cope as a couple. Know that you will be a better parent and partner because you took time to care for yourself. Nurture your relationship with your spouse. It is essential that you have a strong bond to ease the challenges that deafness brings. All will be accomplished more readily if you work as a team.

Parents of newly diagnosed children are immediately aware that their child is different. This difference is now being announced to the world. Suddenly the things that make the child different seem to be enormous. The hearing aids that hang on the side of the head and occasionally buzz become a focus. Parents want to hide the hearing aids and make the deafness go away. Signing in public is a milestone for parents of deaf children. At this point, the hearing aids and the buzzing are no longer important. The parents have come to terms with the reality of the deafness and begun to see a whole child with unique needs.

Enlist the help of trusted family and friends at every level. Encourage them to learn to sign. Some family members may need some encouragement and others will want to jump right in. The more people close to your child who make an effort to sign, the better. Your child will be a more proficient signer because of the reinforcement and a healthier child because of the supportive environment. Allow family and friends to help transport your child to school, therapy sessions, and recreation. Accept financial assistance if available from agencies, university programs (students will often evaluate and work with your child for free), or family. Even with comprehensive medical coverage, your child's needs may become burdensome. Hearing aids, molds, tubes, batteries, audiological exams, and speech therapy are costly.

Most important is yourself. Indeed, this is not the journey that you planned. Do not feel selfish if you are hurt, angry, or depressed. Get help in whatever form is comforting to you. You must address these feelings to move on. However, be aware that these feelings will return as you and your family cope with all the everyday challenges deafness brings. At best, this is a formidable and rewarding adventure and will be for years to come. However, it can also be bittersweet.

You will also need to learn to cope with the outside world. Dealing with the reactions of others to the sounds of your child's voice, to the child's use of hearing aids, or to using sign language in public can be stressful. The look on people's faces can be devastating. Often complete strangers feel they have a right to comment or offer advice.

When Meghan was a baby, a checker in a grocery store called her the "duck," because she squawked. Every time I entered the store, jokes were made about the arrival of the duck. Meghan simply vocalized at this level because it was self-satisfying just as babbling is satisfying for a hearing infant. One day, I left a cart full of groceries and never returned.

I have little patience for people who insult my child

intentionally or not. As a hearing parent, I face so many new issues, responsibilities, and challenges that it really seems unfair that I must also endure the wrath of unenlightened people. The sound a deaf baby makes or the sound of a person's voice is a superficial layer of language and should never be the basis of judgment. However, this aspect of deafness does not go away.

When faced with this situation, I usually turn to a trusted friend. Sometimes a close friend will offer a perspective or suggestion for dealing with the situation that I did not consider. Sometimes validation and an opportunity to vent are all that is necessary.

When a hurtful remark is made by a close friend or family member, I do suggest that you address it. My rule of thumb is that if that individual is going to have an influence or impact on my child's life, in any way at all, then I must take action to educate the person. Because this experience can be wrenching, I wait until my initial anger is resolved so that I can effectively communicate. I initiate conversations with the guilty party with nonthreatening openers, such as, "I've been meaning to talk to you about something," or "Do you have a couple of minutes to listen?" or "I've been thinking about something you said the other day," or "Perhaps I misunderstood the comment you made the other day."

Parents of older deaf or hard-of-hearing children have often said that the feelings of sadness or anger have returned at different times in their children's lives. These feelings can often be as powerful as the feelings experienced at the time of initial diagnosis. Often the feelings pop up when they least expect it. Everything seems to be going fine and then a roadblock is placed in the child's way. It may be something as small as not being included in a party, having to arrange an interpreter so that the child can participate in an event, or a thoughtless remark. It may be something more traumatic such as further loss of hearing or finding out that your child has additional health problems. These feelings always seem to be simmering below the surface. Even parents who are coping very well and are proud and happy with their child's achievements will revisit the feelings of initial diagnosis from time to time.

I marvel with a tinge of jealousy when I watch my hearing friends with their hearing children. Unloading the dishwasher while having a conversation with a child in an adjoining room seems incredible to me. Yet the same friends marvel as we dance through our very special communication system using signs, voice, and visual pictures.

3

~~~~~~

A NEW PATH

This is the journey you must take—make the best of it. Your child will make faster progress if you can take a positive attitude and begin to take action. This journey holds some unique and special rewards. It truly won't matter that your child may sign he loves you long before he voices it.

Our son learned the power of this sign at about eighteen months and wooed countless people. We cheerfully accept our daughter's corrections of our substandard signing skills and her reprimands to practice more. We count these things as our dividends and are moved when we recognize how deafness bonds our family.

Seek out other parents of deaf children. Whether from your child's school, your sign language class, or a doctor's or therapist's office, these people will become an important part of your support system. They have a similar journey and their tales and insight will be refreshing for you. Some of my closest friendships are with other parents of deaf children. Your child and family will benefit from the exposure and companionship of similar families.

Seek out Deaf adults. Our experience is that Deaf adults are willing and eager to share their experiences and knowledge. They will be supportive and sometimes influential in your child's life. Deaf adults can be role models for both you and your child. Deaf adults will teach you about Deaf culture, just by their very presence in your life. Digest and reflect on these cultural points. Remember that you are raising a bicultural child. Your support of your child's culture is essential to his or her self-esteem. Value the unique individual who is your child.

Your reactions to your child's hearing loss will depend on the circumstances surrounding the loss. Some of the factors influencing your circumstances are the age when intervention began, when hearing aids were introduced, the cause of the hearing loss, the amount of residual hearing, and the family's previous experience with deaf or hard-of-hearing people. These factors are different for each child and family. Every family will develop individual coping mechanisms.

I am frequently amazed when I hear of parents who diagnosed their child's hearing loss at six months. Not only am I amazed but it makes me feel guilty. As an educator, I feel I should have figured it out sooner. I am continually reminded that my daughter had virtually no language at two years of age, as I watch my son sign and voice at the same age. How very frustrating that must have been for Meghan, to have a mind as sharp as hers and no communication mode.

Feelings of embarrassment, frustration, anger, hurt, and guilt are not productive, but they are very real and must be addressed. Moving forward in a positive manner will, in the end, reap greater rewards for you and your family. Align yourself with people who feed your soul. Move through this experience with an open mind. Don't get caught up in the inconsequential, superficial pieces. Keep a perspective that possesses energy with a vision to the future success of your child. When you begin to see the deafness as a unique and special experience, you have made an important paradigm shift. It's almost like redefining beauty. You have attached positive attributes to the uniqueness of your child and your child will react to this new paradigm. When children see themselves as successful, they usually are.

Writing can be therapeutic. I have a journal I keep for each of my children. It contains anecdotes of their milestones, situations that were painful and joyful, and the important lessons in parenting they have taught me. I have also put their photographs and little art projects between the pages of their journals. These journals help feed my soul on our more challenging days. They remind me of the progress we've made and the fun we've shared. Perhaps, one day when my children are adults, I will share their journals with them.

This journey will present obstacles and situations you are not prepared for. Do not question your competence or ability. We all do the best we can with who we are and what we've learned. Consider yourself a lifelong learner and gather all the information you can.

One of the things I've frequently heard from well-meaning people is that God doesn't give us more than we can handle or that God is testing me or that God gave me these children for a reason. On some days, these little sayings are of some comfort; on other days, they amuse me (especially when this person has no children of his or her own), and at other times these sayings are trite and annoying. At these times, I really feel like telling the person to tell God to give me a different test. After all, he's given me the same test twice. In essence, you are not just dealing with your child's deafness, you are dealing with the outside world. It is here that I have found some of the greatest challenges. After a

11

friend found out that my daughter was deaf, she called to send her condolences. I found this alarming. After all, Meghan wasn't sick or dying.

Don't hesitate to seek professional counseling. Chances are you may not have had experience with deafness or you may not even know a deaf person. One of the best things you can do for your family is to take care of yourself. Working through your emotions is both physically and emotionally healthy. Soon you will find that a unique rhythm will come to your family and all of this will not seem so shocking or strange. You will be proud of the uniqueness your child brings. You will learn and grow in ways you did not anticipate. Further, you and your family will become role models to the rest of the family and your friends. These people may not have experience with deafness. They will need to learn from you.

My daughter has become aware that frequently people stare at us as we sign and communicate. I reassure her that this is because they are fascinated and interested in our signing. Her frequent response is that they should learn sign language. In our community, she has become somewhat of an ambassador. The fact that Meghan initiates conversations in sign publicly reflects her feelings of competence and completeness.

4

BONDING AND COMMUNICATING

The bond between parent and infant establishes communication styles and expectations for the rest of the child's life. Parents and infants have a way of communicating that is completely nonverbal. This means that words are not used. This nonverbal communication exists on all sensory levels. Parents generally stimulate their infants through visual, auditory, tactile, and kinesthetic modes. The interactions have a rhythmical quality that has been described as a dance between parent and child. All parents and infants have their own style that custom fits their relationship.

It is fascinating to watch this dance. For example, when the child vocalizes, the parent responds by dialoguing. When a baby burps, the parent says, "Oh you burped. Do you feel better now?" Tactually and kinesthetically, this dialogue also exists when the parent holds, rocks, bounces, or soothes the baby. Visual stimulation is perhaps the most important dialogue of all. It conveys intimacy, distance, happiness, or distress. It is the first language that babies understand. Baby smiles are the first result of effective visual dialoguing. Eye-to-eye contact makes mothers feel more comfortable with their babies. It is necessary for language development. Most verbal exchanges between mother and child take place when this mutual gaze occurs. Auditory exchanges develop naturally from the eye-to-eye contact. The dialogue between the parent and baby changes over the first year. The baby's verbalizations increase until the baby is initiating the dialogue.

The child responds to the parents' expressions and body language. Similarly, parents respond to the baby's cries and behaviors to understand what the baby wants. This interactive process is a basis for later communication and cognitive growth. This reciprocity is very important. A balance between parent and child is established. Disruption in this balance may occur when either the parent or the child fails to reciprocate or respond to the other's cues. For example, in cases of neglect, infants do not respond to sensory stimulation in the normal way because reciprocity has not been established. They do not smile, verbalize, reach out, or give good eye contact because they have learned that no one will respond. This bond can also be disrupted when the child does not respond normally to the parent's cues. An example of this is when a child is blind and the parent cannot establish eye contact. The parent has to be taught different ways to establish a bond with the child using other senses such as tactile and auditory.

The disruption that can occur with a deaf child is more subtle. The deaf or hard-of-hearing child uses vision to capture the parent's attention. Parents naturally respond to this dance by emphasizing visual stimulation with the child. The problem occurs when the child does not respond to the auditory and verbal stimulation. As the child gets older, this becomes more apparent. However, sometimes the parents have stopped talking or have limited the way they communicate.

Reciprocity is the exchange of verbal and nonverbal messages. Reciprocity between parent and child extends beyond verbal communication. It is the exchange of visual messages, tactile messages, and verbal messages that bond parent and child. The child's ability to acquire language becomes compromised when reciprocity begins to diminish. In addition, the bond between the parent and child becomes weakened. This lack of reciprocity in the parent-child relationship results in a distance in the relationship. The isolation that can occur in these situations for both parent and child may be confusing and painful.

I observed the mother of a newly diagnosed toddler interacting with her son. As she spoke to her child, the lack of reciprocity in their relationship became apparent. The mother spoke to the child without doing anything to engage the child's attention. The child had no idea that the mother was speaking to him. She did not establish eye contact with the child. She did not touch him or prompt him in any way. The mother spoke to the child while standing across the room from him. The child was seated and engaged in a toy. The mother quickly became frustrated because the child didn't respond the way she expected. The lack of reciprocity between mother and child was deteriorating their bond.

I became increasingly alarmed when my daughter and I were not able to communicate. There was no reciprocity in our relationship. She did not respond to any spoken language. I knew somewhere in this dance we were failing to connect. After Meghan was diagnosed and we began signing, her communication soared. At twenty-seven months, she came home anxiously signing a sign that I did not recognize. Later, the teacher (the co-author of this book), informed me that she was signing, "Pay attention!" Reciprocity, needless to say, was then more fully established.

5

PARENTS ARE TEACHERS

Parents are their children's first teachers. Although they are not trained to teach their child language, they are inherently qualified for this task. Distinct characteristics of language are used by most parents. Hearing parents use strategies that elicit oral language, whereas many Deaf parents use strategies that elicit sign language. This natural way of communicating with a baby is universal throughout the world and these characteristics are similar in many different languages. The parents use these strategies without thinking, unless something has happened to disturb the natural reciprocity of the relationship.

The following examples illustrate parent language strategies. The first example illustrates strategies that hearing parents use when communicating with their babies. The second example refers to strategies that Deaf parents use.

Hearing Parents' Communication Strategies
- Parents and babies engage in prolonged gazing at each other.
- Parents use an abundance of nonverbal communication, facial expression, and gestures.
- The pitch of the parents' voices in baby conversations is higher and exaggerated intonation patterns are used.

- Parents use short and simple grammatically correct sentences.

- Parents use key words and phrases and repeat them.

- Parents talk about the concrete, the here and now, whatever the child is seeing or doing.

- Parents ask many questions as a way of describing a child's activities or behavior, for example, "Are you eating peaches?"

- Parents imitate, interpret, and encourage the child to vocalize. When a baby says "ma," mothers conclude that the baby is saying "Mom."

- Parents allow for response time. They wait for the baby's response.

Deaf Parents' Communication Strategies

- Parents position their bodies to maximize the child's attention.

- Parents make certain that they have their child's visual attention before signing.

- Parents use different sensory modalities to communicate: visual, kinesthetic, auditory.

- Parents frequently sign on the child's face and body.

- Parents sign on objects to make the association clear.

- Parents show the object they want to talk about.

- Parents use pointing (up to 50 percent of their signing).

- Parents frequently sign one-handed when doing chores or holding the baby.

- Parents exaggerate the size of signs and repeat the movement of the sign.

- Parents hold and move the child's hands to form a sign when playing with the child.

- Parents allow for response time. They wait for the baby's response.

- Sentences are short and simple.

- Parents exaggerate signs that produce a visual picture such as a boat in the water or an airplane flying in the sky.

These communication strategies are important to all babies and serve many purposes. Parents will want to use strategies that promote the child's acquisition of language. Parents who use these strategies promote positive and pleasurable feelings. By paying attention to a child's needs and interests, children learn to interact and talk about what they are doing. It is essential to promote your child's interest in communication.

Hearing parents of deaf children can use these strategies to help their deaf or hard-of-hearing child communicate. Both hearing and Deaf parents use eye contact as an essential strategy in developing communication. However, hearing parents of deaf or hard-of-hearing children must be sure to get the child's full attention by positioning the child appropriately and establishing eye contact before initiating communication. Deaf parents allow the children to explore the materials or toys before asking for attention and communication. Both visual exploration and physical manipulation are important. They cue the child's attention to an activity and peak the child's interest. Hearing parents can talk to a hearing child as the child explores and manipulates. The child does not have to be focused on the speech to understand and benefit. However, a deaf or hard-of-hearing child needs to have attention focused on communication in order for the deaf child to benefit from the language interaction.

This focusing of attention on language is the most important thing that you can learn about communicating with your deaf or hard-of-hearing child. You must make a conscious effort to stop and attend to what you are saying to the child. This makes communication more difficult for the hearing parent and it takes more time. However, the benefits of early communication, bonding with your child, and establishing a rhythm of communication will stay with your child for the rest of his or her life.

Hearing parents must be sure that they position the child so that face-to-face communication is optimum. Get down at eye level and connect with the child in a tactile way by continuously touching the child in a comforting way. This touch prompts the child to attend to the communication. Use a motivating object or toy to arouse the child's curiosity. When you want the child to look at your face, put the toy next to your face but not covering your mouth. Let's use a red ball as an example. As you say "Look," bring the ball to the side of your face. As soon as the child is engaged or shows good eye contact, repeat the word "ball" several times and sign around the ball. Give the ball to the child. Allow the child to explore and manipulate the toy, all the while signing and saying the word "ball." Manipulate the child's hands to sign the word around the object and immediately use positive reinforcement: clap, or kiss or hug the child. Expand the communication by talking about the properties and what the ball can do. The ball is red, round, soft, or hard. Throw the ball up and say, "Up, up, up!" Associate a sound with the object that can be used for auditory training. For example, drop the ball on the floor and say "Uh, oh." Use short, simple sentences with distinct intonation patterns. Exaggerate the sign visually to catch the child's attention. Encourage the child to vocalize and sign. Remember to wait and give the child a chance to respond. Continue to positively respond to any attempt the child makes to communicate.

Accept and encourage any gesture, sign, or vocalization that your child offers. Do not get discouraged or compare your child's ability to another child the same age. Celebrate your child knowing that this is a precious time. Allow yourself the luxury of enjoying this playful time with your child. One of the most vital lessons I've learned raising two deaf children is the importance of being a mom. It is more important than being a speech therapist or a teacher. I leave the drill and practice to another professional. My time with my children is better spent in allowing their personalities to emerge and flourish.

6

▼▼▼

EXTENDED FAMILY MEMBERS

Your child's hearing loss will have an impact on all family members. Some extended family members will intrinsically know that the bond with your child will include communicating in sign language. They will come along immediately with their support. The bond with these family members will be deepened and they will make your child's deafness a joyful experience. Other family members will have a more challenging time appreciating the diversity that your child brings to the family. Although wanting to be supportive, they may become intimidated by the impact the disability holds for them. These family members will need to work through a process of accepting and understanding deafness.

One reaction to the deafness is pity manifested in statements such as "I feel so sorry for you," or "The poor little deaf child..." Dwelling in pity slows progress for both your child and you. You may be feeling sorry for yourself and it may be comforting to play this role for awhile. However, feeling sorry for yourself or your child will damage your child's self-esteem. The message you give your child, perhaps even unconsciously, is that there is something dreadfully wrong with him or her.

Many times, this pity is based on outdated information and low expectations for your child. I remember a family member was surprised to find a Deaf adult who not only drove a car, but was an engineer. Appropriate doses of information regarding the abilities of deaf children and adults may counteract feelings of pity and give such onlookers a more realistic perspective.

Well-intentioned extended family members can also be hurtful while considering themselves supportive. They may try to protect you by ignoring or minimizing the hearing loss. Often they are embarrassed about the disability or feel uncomfortable around the hearing aids or signing. To them, such aids and use of sign language are a jarring advertisement of the deafness. This reflects their own insecurities about how to best deal with the situation.

Again, education or a sense of humor may be your best ally. Educate these extended family members but don't overwhelm them with information. Realize that it may take awhile for them to understand and appreciate the diversity that your child brings to the family. Observing you and how you interact with your child may be the most powerful tool you have. Sharing a laugh about a funny situation you have encountered with deafness may help release some of the tension. While taking a walk one day, Meghan asked if the cows in the field were meowing. It struck us as humorous that of course a deaf child really wouldn't know if a cow was mooing or meowing.

The etiology of the hearing loss can often become the source of tension in the extended family. Comments about the etiology of the hearing loss such as "It couldn't have come from our family," or "If you hadn't worked outside the home during your pregnancy..." can be extremely hurtful and anger provoking. Parents may already carry their share of guilt. These comments can cause huge rifts in families.

Open communication regarding the etiology of the hearing loss and your feelings regarding these statements is essential. Make "I" statements when broaching this subject. For example say, "I feel really hurt when you suggest that I caused my child's hearing loss," or "I feel really hurt when you state the hearing loss must be from the other side of the family." This is a particularly delicate situation for both you and extended family members. The spouse whose family is having difficulty may have to sit down with the family members and have a heart-to-heart talk.

Remember to stay focused on your child. Weigh the importance of your child having a relationship with this extended family member. Does he or she live in town and have continual contact with your child or does the individual only see your child once a year at holidays? Put yourself on the line and address the situation if this extended family member is going to play an important role in your child's life. If you only see this person occasionally, you may not want to put forth the emotional effort to change his attitude.

Another source of tension is often family holiday gatherings. Many times the deaf or hard-of-hearing children are overwhelmed by the noise and confusion, especially if no one is making an effort to sign. Deaf children in these situations become isolated in a roomful of people. Consider how you seat people at holiday gatherings. Make sure that your child is near someone who will sign and be a comfort to him or her. If you are busy at a family gathering, make sure that your child has access to someone who will help him or her be a part of the group.

Extended family members can be a source of tremendous support. Many will engage themselves learning about deafness and signing. They will consider this an opportunity for new learning. Furthermore, cousins and other children in the family may find that learning signs is an exciting new way to communicate.

Meghan and Sean's cousins boast about the deafness in the family, showing off their sign skills to their friends. They cannot wait until the children visit to practice and learn more signs. On one occasion, Meghan and Sean went to school for "show and tell" to teach a cousin's class sign language.

Extended family members can also provide relief and support. They may be willing to help with transporting your child to appointments, or by baby-sitting, or even by providing financial support. Take advantage of these opportunities. Many extended family members find satisfaction in participating and playing a pivotal role in your child's life. Allow them this pleasure.

Don't expect all family members to be on the same time line. Try to exercise patience with extended family members who resist or are uncomfortable with the family changes that deafness brings. Some people are set in their beliefs and attitudes and are not open to new information and change. Attempt to avoid family rifts regarding deafness. The message these rifts give your child is not emotionally healthy. Your reward for exercising patience in these situations may be eventual understanding and harmony in the extended family.

7

CONNECTING BROTHERS AND SISTERS

Connecting brothers and sisters in any family can be a challenge. When another factor such as deafness is thrown into the relationship, more obstacles appear. Deafness is a communication barrier that affects sibling relationships. Parents need to bond brothers and sisters so that communication doesn't limit the interactions of siblings.

In a family where both children are deaf, fewer obstacles are present. Jealousy from either the hearing or the deaf child is not an issue. The family has firmly established a communication system when the second child arrives. The arrival of a second deaf child may be heart wrenching for the parents. However, the older deaf child often reacts with joy. Parents should follow this example. These siblings will always have a very special bond, their deafness. In fact, the older sibling may be proud that the second child was born deaf. She is excited to see someone in the family like herself. No longer is the family different because of one deaf member. The family is redesigned. It has a unique balance of both deaf and hearing members. Parents are more equipped the second time around, allowing siblings to flourish in an environment suited to their needs.

Connect brothers and sisters in meaningful ways early. The bond they share will be the foundation for a lifelong relationship.

The balance in families when just one family member has a hearing loss is more delicate. Some problems can develop between siblings because of one child's deafness. This may be the result of a variety of factors such as poor communication, inconsistent discipline, difficulty in interactions between siblings, or jealousy. Attention to these factors will help to establish a stronger family unit.

A hearing sibling may feel that the parents are showering too much attention on the deaf child's needs. Let's face it, deaf children do take more time. The hearing child needs to feel special, one of a kind, and a unique part of the family. If you must take your hearing child to some of the deaf child's many appointments, interweave an activity especially for the hearing child. For example, share an ice cream with the hearing child while the deaf child is in a speech lesson. Have the hearing child bring something back as a reward for the deaf child. This will help the bonding process between children.

One of the best ways to bond siblings is to teach them that they are peers. Help your children, whether they are both deaf or one is deaf and one is hearing, to be companions. Encourage cooperative play when siblings are young. Dress-up games are wonderful fun and encourage a child's creativity and individuality. Baking projects are also good interactive sibling activities. Sandboxes, play dough, and train sets also provide the backdrop for interactive fun. As you give your children opportunities to share fun, you will be amazed at how they learn to compensate for the other's special needs. When you program sibling fun in your life, your children will not only remember when they played particular games, they will have lifetime memories of childhood fun. Sibling bonds are deepened through the years as brothers and sisters share memories of family fun.

Many times during cooperative play, a commotion will develop. In these situations, it is recommended that parents don't spend time holding court and deciding who was right and who was wrong. Often it is best for parents to stand back and give the children a chance to work out the problems themselves. Remember that you are trying to develop self-control and positive interactions between siblings. These negotiating skills practiced with siblings at home transfer to the world at large. Generally, all the children are responsible for group misbehavior no matter the age or disability. However, when one child hits another, parental intervention is necessary.

Consistent standards for behavior between siblings, whether deaf or hearing, are necessary. Resentment will build and place a wedge between siblings if standards for behavior are lower for the deaf or hard-of-hearing child. Resentment will also build if the hearing child must continually play the role of parent. Don't expect your hearing child to be responsible for disciplining or constantly interpreting for your deaf child. Certainly in the outside world, your hearing child may be an advocate for your deaf child, but peer bonding depends on mutual respect.

Another issue that frequently emerges in families with both hearing and deaf children is setting standards for signing in the family. Allow hearing children times and places where they are free to express themselves through oral language exclusively. These children must also feel unique and have opportunities for encouragement to communicate freely by voice. Set standards that allow for flexibility so that hearing children want to sign but don't feel coerced to sign. One family established a rule that you had to sign in the kitchen and family room. This was where the family gathered. This gave hearing children flexibility to use their voices in their own space such as their bedroom.

Deaf or hard-of-hearing children may need guidance to appropriately resolve conflicts with words. Sometimes, due to a lack of communication prowess, deaf children may resort to physical action. Model appropriate behavior and language for resolving conflicts. Give your deaf child specific words and phrases for interacting appropriately, such as, "Excuse me," "It's my turn," "Wait until I'm finished," "I want —," and " I don't want —." Encourage children to exercise more control over the situation. Deaf children may need extra help in understanding and participating in games. To avoid conflicts, make sure they are clear about the rules.

Deaf and hearing children are much more alike than different. Everything from board games to sports are appropriate activities for siblings to enjoy together. There should be no limit to the fun that your deaf and hearing children share. Occasionally, an incident will arise that illustrates the difference. Accommodations must be made when games or interactions include noise as a trigger. This can be frustrating for a deaf child because he or she feels left out of the loop. For example, a flashlight or scarf may be substituted for a bell or whistle or other noise so that a deaf child can participate fully.

Jealousy between deaf and hearing siblings may also arise as the deaf child realizes that the world is full of sounds that he or she is unable to hear. While camping, Joel, a hard-of-hearing child, was confused by the sounds he heard. His new hearing aids allowed him to hear a steady chirping noise. When he asked his brothers about this irritating noise, they laughingly informed him it was the sound that crickets made. Joel was astonished and taken aback to learn that these small insects could make such a noise. Children in these situations feel as though they've been left out and sometimes will become angry.

Diffusing these types of situations is truly a challenge. It brings forth the difference and forces us to try to deal with a situation we can't solve. This is a part of the deafness and it is a reality we must face. It isn't fair and we as parents can't always make things better. These obstacles can make us feel somewhat fragile and inadequate. Stay focused on a vision of the future and realize that some of the pieces of this journey are bittersweet.

8

~~~~~~

A TRANQUIL HOME

Environments filled with tension affect children, their emotional well-being, and their learning. Classroom interruptions are not only costly wastes of time but cause a deficit in the environment that is difficult to reinstate. A teacher can often tell when something is wrong at home by observing a child's behavior. Children who are from stable home environments show it in their learning behaviors. They are on task, self-directed, and confident learners. Occasionally, such a child comes to school in a blue mood and you realize how the home environment affects a student's performance. In the best of circumstances, this only happens occasionally and students can be brought back to a positive place where learning can proceed. However, occasionally students come to us from homes where tension is high and limits have not been set. These students inevitably have slower rates of learning.

Chances are, as a hearing parent of a deaf or hard-of-hearing child, your life since the birth of your child and his or her diagnosis has been intense. Securing the medical and educational attention your child needs has been time consuming, financially burdening, and emotionally traumatic. Informing family members and friends and dealing with their reactions may have taken a further toll on your emotional wellness. This is all a part of the challenge you face. Indeed, you may be in turmoil at times. Try to release some of this burden in positive ways: exercise, lunch with a friend, or get a facial or massage. Think of activities that are relaxing and fulfilling for you personally. Believe it or not, your emotional state has everything to do with your child's behavior. Infants react to levels of tension in the home. Infants who have been subjected continually to tension-filled environments develop coping mechanisms that include negative attention-getting behaviors. As the infant grows, these behaviors are amplified and get in the way of establishing relationships with others and learning at a normal rate. The first step in establishing positive behavior in your child is by establishing a tranquil home environment. You set the weather in your home. Your disposition and mood are the first and foremost factors in creating a home that nurtures your child as a whole and creates positive feelings and behaviors in the child. Let your style of parenting come through. Establish a tone in your home that feels good to you and this will inevitably feel good to your child.

Establishing a home environment that is nurturing and positive includes setting limits. If you don't set limits, your child will set his or her own. These limits need to be appropriate for your child's developmental age. The first step in setting limits begins with situations that are dangerous. Baby-proof your home. It is far easier to create an environment where your child is free to explore and play in safety than to follow your baby or toddler continually signing and shouting, "No!" At this age, confine your discipline to situations that are dangerous such as the oven or fireplace.

Do not hesitate to set limits for your child. This means that when you say "No," you mean "No." Think before you speak. If you as a parent change the rules in response to your child's whining or crying, you are only teaching your child that whining and crying are good ways to get what he or she wants. Children often want to do things that are not good for them such as watch too much TV, stay up late, and eat whatever they want. Parents need to take control of young children's lives to make sure they are safe, get enough sleep, eat properly, and spend time playing creatively. Children cannot always have what they want and the sooner they learn this life lesson, the better. If you do not take control of these situations when your children are small, you will not be able to control them when they become teenagers.

Young deaf or hard-of-hearing children who do not have effective ways of telling their parents what they want will often just go and get what they want. They will also frequently fall into tantrums when they cannot make themselves understood. Hearing parents often feel helpless to control the child's behavior because the child does not understand the language that the parent is using to set the limits. The parent feels sorry for the child and makes allowances because the child is deaf. This can create real problems in the family especially if other siblings feel they are being treated differently than the deaf child.

There is no one way to discipline all children at all times. Your personality and parenting style will play an important role in how you discipline your child. My limits are different from my friends and siblings, as they should be. For instance, I never insist that my daughter go to bed by herself. This may seem extremely lenient and as though there is no limit. However, my daughter is very frightened of the dark and panics when left alone in a dark place, even a place as familiar as her own bedroom. At night when she is not wearing her hearing aids and cannot see through the darkness she becomes very agitated. We therefore try to establish a positive routine and help her adjust instead of reprimanding her. Limit setting in such a situation would damage a child's self-esteem.

9

MEDICAL PROFESSIONALS

Most deaf or hard-of-hearing children do not appear delayed in their development when they are under three years of age. Many hearing children do not talk much at this age especially in a situation outside their home. It often seems as if the deaf child is just as competent as his or her hearing peers. However, often the deaf child is deficient in language, whereas the hearing child understands what is said to him or her.

Deafness is a disability that is hidden and this can often cause parents to delay making the commitment to face the issues and seek out help. Furthermore, many medical professionals and even well-meaning friends and family will assure you that everything is all right. Deafness is a low-incidence disability and many pediatricians never see a congenitally deaf child. The law of averages is on the doctor's side when he tells you not to be concerned about a child who is delayed in developing speech. It is essential for parents to advocate for their child.

The first professionals that you will meet and work with will be from the medical community. The doctor will be the person who will diagnose your child. The pediatrician, ENT (ear, nose, and throat specialist), and audiologist will bring valuable information to the medical team. Do not be intimidated by the professionals you meet. Do not be afraid to ask questions. Seeking information is how you are going to cope with this new reality. You need to understand what is going on to make good decisions and care for your child.

Many parents report that the initial diagnosis was a traumatic experience. Remember that you know your child better than anyone else in the world. You know your child as a person, not a medical problem. Your perspective on your child provides vital information to the medical team. You are a key player on the team. Trust your instincts. If you are not getting the answers that you need or if you are not comfortable with the team, the team may not be working for you. You will need to keep looking for medical professionals who support you.

The first labels applied to your child will come from the medical community. You may hear words such as handicapped, disabled, hearing impaired, hard-of-hearing, or deaf. Do not be frightened by these stereotypical labels. They hold much impact because they are new and most people have preconceived notions about what these words mean. Don't allow labels to become emotional roadblocks. Labels you receive from the medical community will actually pave the way to secure services for your child.

The focus of the medical team is to come up with an accurate diagnosis and a prescription that will include the best possible amplification for your child. Obtaining appropriate hearing aids is the first step in assisting your child. Educate yourself. Become partners with your medical team. Read as much as you can and take advantage of what modern technology offers.

It is very important for parents to realize that no one professional can give you all the answers. These people can be your allies and help you understand the special needs of your deaf or hard-of-hearing child. However, you, as the parent, are ultimately responsible for your child's development and you have to make the hard decisions. It will be helpful to understand who these professionals are, what their background and training is, and what their perspective is. This information will help you evaluate advice that they give you. Following is a list of medical professionals you will encounter.

Pediatrician: a medical doctor who sees to the general health needs of your child. Not a specialist.

Audiologist: a specialist in the science of hearing who administers audiometric tests and contributes to the rehabilitative process by prescribing appropriate amplification. Some audiologists also sell hearing aids.

Pediatric Audiologist: an audiologist who specializes in testing and prescribing amplification for children.

Neurologist: a medical doctor whose specialty is the brain and central nervous system.

Otolaryngoloist: a medical doctor whose specialty is the general area of the ear, nose, and throat.

Otologist/ENT: a medical doctor whose specialty is confined solely to hearing and hearing specialty.

Hearing Aid Dealer: a salesperson who sells hearing aids prescribed by an audiologist. Responsible for monitoring the function of the hearing aids. Not a medical doctor or an educator.

There is so much for you to do once your child is diagnosed with a hearing loss. The process and interaction with so many medical professionals can overwhelm anyone. New labels and huge quantities of unfamiliar medical information will inevitably cause confusion. It is essential that you stay focused on sifting through the medical advice. Keep on track in securing the medical services necessary for your child. This medical information provides the scaffolding for further learning. It is essential to understand the medical information so that you can move forward.

The medical community views a hearing loss as a medical problem to be fixed. The medical professionals will provide essential information, technology, and assistance. Many doctors will also provide emotional support and be a calming force during this tumultuous time.

10

DEAF COMMUNITY

The Deaf community can provide your family with an array of resources. You can tap some of these resources at schools for the deaf, city recreational programs, community colleges, and deaf organizations. Don't feel intimidated to reach out to the Deaf community. A good place to begin is by attending workshops and in-services for parents and educators of deaf children. Workshops can provide helpful information and connect you with other parents and professionals. Even if you choose to fully include your child in a neighborhood public school, you may appreciate the contact with Deaf role models and information provided at a workshop. Usually many points of view are represented and you may find books or other materials that will have updated information.

Some cities provide recreational programs for deaf or hard-of-hearing students. Your child may enjoy a recreational activity tailored for deaf children and the opportunity to socialize with other deaf children. Swim lessons with an instructor familiar with deaf children is an activity you may want to consider. Many summer camps are available for deaf children and their families. These programs and camps can be wonderful for a deaf child's self-esteem. Find out what is available in your area and observe the activities. Deaf families often participate in these activities. These are great places to connect with Deaf role models for your child and to establish support systems for your family.

Schools for the deaf may also have programs that may interest your deaf child. Sports teams that have several deaf members allow your child to participate in an environment that is less intimidating and more relaxing. Soccer and bowling teams are sports that many deaf children enjoy. Besides sports programs, investigate classes that may develop a unique competence in your child. Extracurricular clubs and hobbies are wonderful means of supporting a child's particular interest. Many times, Deaf adults are interested and support these activities as leaders or as parents themselves.

Churches in your area may also have programs for the deaf. Research church services and dramatic productions with interpreters. Sometimes even classes and workshops designed for deaf members will be available. Frequently, interpreters are provided for church services and children's programs. These kinds of social situations are perfect for interacting and meeting Deaf adults in your community and may also serve your own needs for personal growth.

With my son in his stroller, I attended a conference where I met many Deaf adults. They continually besieged us and admired and enjoyed my son. Repeatedly I was told how amazing and beautiful his baby signs were. What amazed me was the effect that such tremendous positive reinforcement had on a baby younger than age two. He replied with his entire repertoire of language. I, too, was inspired and lifted by the experience. He was so excited by so many people using signs to communicate with him that he was never afraid when surrounded by strangers. The Deaf adults accepted this child as a long lost family member. They encouraged me to continue to sign with my child. I was reassured that the path we had chosen, using both signing and speech, for our children was the appropriate one.

Although a doctor may have a lot of medical knowledge, he does not know what it feels like to be a deaf person and may not know what a deaf person would want. It is more important to listen to someone who has experienced a similar situation as your child.

As a parent, you know your child as a competent unique individual. Deafness is an integral part of your child's whole being. Your child will always be deaf and this will bring its special rewards and challenges. Searching out individuals in the Deaf community who have a positive attitude toward deafness will create a more balanced view of your child. The Deaf community sees a language difference, not a medical problem, and can provide information and emotional support.

11

EDUCATIONAL PROFESSIONALS

A team approach is most effective when planning an educational program for your child. It is important to have advice from a variety of disciplines and educational professionals. The parent is the most important person on the educational team. Parents bring valuable information about the child's development and learning style. Teamwork doesn't just happen. It takes effort on both sides. Developing a good partnership with your child's teachers means listening and learning from each other.

There are many things you can do to establish positive teamwork with educational professionals. Keep a list of items you want to discuss. Being prepared will show that you respect each professional's time. A list of questions will also help you focus on what is important to you. Repeat what you hear in your own words to be sure that you really understand what has been said. This will also help the professionals explain things more clearly. You can use phrases such as "Let me see if I have got this straight ..." or "Did you mean that ..." Don't be embarrassed if you get it wrong. Asking questions, assembling information so that it makes sense, and rephrasing new information are excellent strategies.

The educational professionals will be interested in your child's behavior, developmental progress, and interactions at home. Keep logs of your child's reactions to different situations. Note milestones, no matter how small they may seem. Observe your child playing independently and cooperatively, and make notes. Notice which toys your child plays with most frequently and what kind of play he prefers. Keep a record of the communication your child attempts. This includes nonverbal communication such as pointing, shaking his head, and facial expression. Write down new signs and words. Note activities that prove to be challenging or overwhelm your child. This log does not need to be formal. Keep a journal on the kitchen counter and jot down items as they occur. This type of information will assist educational professionals in determining your child's preferred style of learning and in establishing appropriate goals.

The focus of the educational team is to assess your child to determine strengths and needs and to plan an educational program. The educational professionals should be trained in deaf education and understand the implications of a hearing loss. Here is a list of some of the educational professionals that you will meet.

Teacher of the Deaf: educator trained in strategies and methodologies for teaching deaf and hard-of-hearing children. Familiar with the controversies in the field regarding the use of sign language and auditory/oral approach and generally trained in one method or the other.

School Administrator/Site Principal: oversees the curriculum and educational needs of students. Supervises teachers and other staff members. May or may not have a background in deaf education.

Speech Pathologist: specially trained in strategies and methodologies for developing speech production and language skills. May have educational or clinical background. May or may not have experience working with deaf children.

Paraprofessional/Teacher Aide: a noncertificated staff member who assists the teacher. The majority of training is on the job. Education and experiential levels vary widely.

Sign Language Interpreter: an individual who has studied sign language or become proficient in sign language. Some have passed formal testing and are certified as sign language interpreters. Generally have no formal training in education techniques.

School Psychologist: a psychologist trained in assessment and testing. This professional helps teachers develop educational plans appropriate to the child's learning style. Also assists teachers in working with behavior problems and developing behavior plans. Many do not have a background in deaf education.

Educational Audiologist: an audiologist who works in an educational setting. Monitors the hearing aids and auditory training equipment of students. Consults with teachers concerning the listening environment in the classroom and often does auditory training.

Occupational/Physical Therapist: a therapist who specializes in assessing and remediating fine and gross motor skills or daily living skills such as feeding. Some deaf and hard-of-hearing children qualify for this service when they have delays in these areas.

Adapted Physical Education (APE) Teacher: a physical education teacher trained to remediate mild gross motor delays. For example, some deaf or hard-of-hearing children have balance problems. The APE specialist will provide activities to work on balance.

Mainstream Teacher/Full Inclusion Teacher: a regular education teacher who has a special education student in his or her classroom. Does not have a background in deaf education. Generally a special education teacher will provide some support to the mainstream teacher. In programs using sign language, sign interpreters are provided. Note takers can also be provided.

Quality education begins and ends with parental support. Most school staff welcome the support and participation of parents at all levels. Besides attending meetings and parent-teacher conferences, become a participating member of the school community. Attend parent support groups, PTA meetings, the school site council, and social functions. Connect with other parents and school staff. If possible, volunteer in your child's classroom. Involving yourself in your child's school will provide a valuable service, give your child positive messages about the importance of education, and administer your child with a healthy dose of self-esteem.

Every professional you meet, both medical and educational, may give different opinions and advice. Some professionals encourage the use of sign language. Others encourage focusing on listening and speech exclusively. This conflicting advice can become confusing. As the parent, you are the leader of the team when it comes to your child. Trust your instincts and make choices with confidence.

I truly had wanted someone to lead me through the work ahead, giving me all the answers, making all the decisions, and dealing with all the challenges that deafness was bringing. I had wanted a fairy godmother to wave her magic wand and make things all right. There were professionals who wanted to take on this role and were willing to tell me exactly what to do. However, I began to realize that blindly following the advice of one person would be an easy way out. After feeling sorry for myself for awhile, I came to grips with the fact that I was not going to be saved from this. I needed to do the hard work for myself as well as for Meghan. My fairy godmother was not going to show up.

12

〰〰〰〰〰〰〰〰〰〰〰〰〰〰〰〰〰〰〰〰〰〰〰〰〰〰〰〰〰〰〰

EDUCATIONAL PLANS

A s soon as your child is diagnosed with a hearing loss, contact the special education department of your local school district. Personnel will be able to refer you to programs available in your area. Your local school district is responsible for providing a free and appropriate education for your child at age three. Agencies responsible for the education of infants and toddlers vary in different areas. However, your local special education director should know what is available in your area. Seek out other parents who have been through the process and get their advice. As a parent of a deaf child, you are guaranteed certain rights. These rights are discussed in Key 14.

Enroll your child in a special education program as soon as possible. An Early Intervention Program generally serves children and families from birth to three years. The Individualized Family Service Plan (IFSP) is a document that is designed to identify your family's strengths and needs. This plan will be reviewed at least every six months. Public Law 94-457, passed in 1986, recognizes that to help a young child, the family must be helped as well. The focus is, therefore, the family and not just the child. The law lists services that should be available to young children and families. These include family training, specialized instruction, speech therapy, audiology, nutrition services, physical therapy, and occupational therapy.

Your family will be assigned a family service coordinator who will manage your child's program. Your family will receive the services that the team identifies as a need for the child and family. You are a full partner on this team. It is important that you share your concerns and goals for your child. It is the job of the team members to develop a plan to help you reach these goals. These services can take place in a variety of settings—your home, a day care center, or a center-based program.

Many Early Intervention Programs are designed for children with a variety of special needs and children at risk. Many teachers in these programs are developmental specialists. Make sure that the program you select for your deaf child has personnel who are trained in working with deaf and hard-of-hearing children. A teacher of the deaf who understands the unique needs of deaf children should provide services to you and your child. A deaf or hard-of-hearing child needs to have a unique program including speech, listening, and language training. The teacher needs to understand your child's audiogram, the hearing aids, and the child's residual hearing, as well as how to plan a listening and speech program based on this information. In addition, the teacher needs to understand the complexities of language learning for deaf children and the myriad of choices that are available to parents. Teachers using signs should be signing with fluency, using a developmental level appropriate to your child.

The private sector may also offer programs in your area. These can be costly. However, you may feel that your child needs some extra individual work to maximize his or her potential. Speech and listening skills development are usually the extra services parents want for their child. Some medical insurance plans will cover all or partial expenses.

Work closely with your insurance company to take advantage of the resources available to you. If your plan does not cover these services, contact your physician and see if he or she can advocate for your child.

Other agencies may also be helpful. Often sign language classes are taught through adult education or junior colleges. Many parent organizations will be able to direct you to services or support groups in your area. Your service coordinator should be able to direct you to community resources.

When your child turns three years old, your school district becomes responsible for your child's education. At this time, you will write a new plan called an Individualized Educational Program (IEP). Once a year, the IEP team meets to plan a program for your child. Although the family continues to be important, the student becomes the focus of the plan. The team members include your child's special education teacher, an administrator or designee, and other professionals working with your child, such as a speech therapist. If your child is included in a regular classroom, the regular education teacher will also be invited.

Following the assessment process, the parents, teachers, specialist, and administrator and, if appropriate, the child, meet to develop the IEP, which will include such specifics as what a child's school day will look like, and whether the child will spend part or all of the day in a regular classroom or in a special education classroom. Other services will be specified in the IEP such as audiology, speech, and language or listening. The IEP will also include the child's current levels of performance and short-term and annual goals and objectives. In many cases, the person responsible for meeting the specific goals or objectives may be listed. A projected date for initiation of the services along with the anticipated evaluation procedures and time lines for evaluation will be listed.

The needs of your deaf child are multidimensional. An appropriate education may include a variety of support services such as audiology, speech therapy, adaptive physical education, and psychological services. Remember that all these services may be an integral part of your child's IEP and will incur no cost to you.

The IEP meeting is designed so that all the participants, including the parent, participate in planning the program. The first part of the IEP discusses your child's current level of performance and your child's strengths and weaknesses. Goals and objectives are written that outline the educational plan for your child. Finally, the services that are needed to complete the plan are listed in the IEP.

The IEP should be a road map that all team members refer to frequently. The team formally meets once a year. However, do not hesitate to contact the other team members between IEP meetings for informal progress reports and to share information. The IEP will be a more valuable document if it is used as the guide for the collective vision the IEP team holds for your child.

13

SCHOOLS AND CLASSROOMS THAT WORK

Educational options for deaf students vary widely; however, several characteristics will be evident in any quality program for the deaf. As you visit programs, you may want to bring this book and review some of the following points.

Are teachers trained in communication techniques and strategies for language learning that will be effective with deaf students? The services of a special teacher of the deaf are of crucial importance whether a deaf child is in a special day class or residential program or fully included in a regular classroom. If a child is fully included in a regular program, a qualified resource person who is a teacher of the deaf is necessary on site to advise and consult with the regular classroom teacher. This resource person can help with the successful integration of a deaf child by giving feedback to the regular classroom teacher and monitoring fully included deaf students closely. A deaf student, whose major concern may be fitting in, will not tell the classroom teacher in a room full of peers that the lesson was not understandable because the teacher turned toward the blackboard when speaking. Indeed, it can be intimidating for anyone to say, "I didn't understand" in a room full of peers.

A resource person for the deaf should have credentials to teach deaf and hard-of-hearing students. This teacher must be accepted and well received by the deaf children in the fully included program. The deaf children must feel connected to this person in order to share concerns, questions, and feelings. Your child is entitled to such a service by federal law.

Does the program have knowledgeable supervisors? Whatever educational option you choose, principals and other supervisors or managers must be knowledgeable in order to manage and maintain a program that serves and meets the needs of deaf students. A knowledgeable supervisor collects data, evaluates and modifies the program and personnel, steers teacher training and professional development, is an instructional leader, and oversees other programs on campus such as parent support groups.

In mainstream or full inclusion classrooms, where the teacher does not sign, deaf students are entitled to interpreters whose service is paid for by the district. An interpreter can be a fabulous asset for deaf children fully included in regular programs. Many deaf children in these situations are delighted to have an interpreter accompany them not just for communication but for academic and social purposes. Others find it offensive particularly as the child gets older. With an interpreter, a deaf child can communicate and participate in discussion readily. Academically, an interpreter allows deaf students a visual mode for learning language and concepts.

A few words of warning regarding interpreters. Some children feel self-conscious about being accompanied in class by an interpreter. Other children begin to rely on the interpreter as much as the classroom teacher. The teacher can even fall into this trap by addressing the interpreter rather than the student. In these cases, take time to meet with the child, interpreter, and teacher. An informal meeting may help everyone get the most from an interpreter's service. Also, in classrooms where hearing peers are not accustomed to an interpreter, a few sessions on the role of the interpreter may be helpful. This can be done by anyone trained in the use of the interpreter. It is important to make sure that the deaf child, classroom teacher, and all students are comfortable with and making appropriate use of the interpreter.

Is appropriate curriculum and instructional equipment readily available? Does the curriculum used meet the developmental and language needs of the deaf child? In cohesive educational programs, similar curricula and teaching strategies are used by all of the teachers in the program. This allows for continuity and reinforcement of concepts. Deaf children need this type of familiarity to retain and apply information learned. Good curriculum is at an instructional level that allows the deaf child to work independently at times, cooperatively with peers at times, and with teacher guidance at other times. Good curriculum, especially in the area of literature, reflects the students' interests, experiences, and culture. Does the class read stories about deaf children and adults? Caption videos and films are a must in a classroom with even one deaf child. Amplification devices such as FM systems may also be necessary. Overhead projectors and visuals such as charts, diagrams, graphs, models, and language or word lists to facilitate writing are all necessary instructional equipment and components of a quality program for a deaf child.

Are deaf children fully included in the school and classroom environment? This environment must be closely evaluated in a program with deaf children. Is it a safe environment? Do the deaf children understand the rules, routines, and announcements of the school? Are these only announced over the loudspeaker or are they interpreted and visually accessible to students? Are school assemblies well managed and do they include an interpreter? Do the deaf children understand the procedures and purpose of fire, earthquake, and other disaster drills? Alarms in the school must have lights, and deaf children need to have the drill procedures modeled correctly. Sensitivity to these issues provides deaf children with safety and an important connection to the school. When deaf children have access to and have internalized the rules, routines, and procedures of the school, they have an increased sense of belonging.

Classrooms with deaf children should have arrangements that are conducive to visual learning. Deaf children need visual access to the other children, the teacher, and the interpreter if appropriate. Sitting in rows is not an acceptable seating arrangement. Arcs, semicircles, and cooperative groups of up to five or six students are more suitable. Lighting is also important. Glare makes lip reading difficult and limits deaf student access to the teacher, other students, and the interpreter.

Noise level is another issue with deaf children. Remember that hearing aids amplify everything. Machines and heating and cooling system noise can create a difficult learning environment for deaf children. Noises that a hearing person naturally tunes out such as radios, compact disc players, telephones, and playground noise may affect a deaf child's ability to focus in the classroom. Sensitivity to these noise issues should be schoolwide.

A well-managed classroom will have students who follow rules regarding when to work independently, and when and how to join a discussion or add a comment or ask a question. The structure and routine of a well-managed classroom allow a deaf child security. Knowing what to expect and how to behave assists the child in focusing on learning. Well-organized and managed classrooms are optimal places for learning.

14

‰‰‰

YOUR RIGHTS

It is your responsibility to secure an appropriate education and advocate for your deaf child. You are guaranteed certain rights in this process. Two laws exist that explicitly define the rights of children and parents.

Public Law 94-457 provides money to states for the provision of educational programs and services to children with exceptional needs from birth to age three. Each state and educational agency must develop a plan with families. There is no national Individualized Family Service Plan (IFSP) form. However, each IFSP must include the following:

- a statement of the child's level of development

- a statement of the family's strengths and needs as they relate to the child's development

- a statement of major outcomes expected for the child and the family, as well as how and when it is hoped they will be achieved

- a statement of which early intervention services are to be provided

- a statement of when services are expected to begin and how long they will continue

- the name of the case manager, the person responsible for carrying out the provisions of the IFSP

- the steps to be taken to help the child transition to a preschool program

The IFSP should use words that make sense to you and reflect the needs of your child and family. This document should encompass a plan to address your family life as it is affected by your child's deafness. Your family will be affected in many ways by your child's deafness. Consider day care and the necessity of having appropriate care providers as you develop the IFSP. Other family needs may include support groups and sign language classes. The IFSP process and the case manager may be valuable assets in getting these needs met.

Under the Individuals with Disabilities Education Act (IDEA; PL94-142) and its recent revision in 1997, all children with disabilities (as determined by the IEP team) are entitled to a free and appropriate public education. It is the responsibility of the local school district to develop an appropriate Individualized Educational Program (IEP). This Federal law entitles deaf children to a free education, adapted to their special needs and equivalent in quality to that available to nondisabled children.

Each school district is required to offer a continuum of placement options for disabled children. One option is attending a special day class program for the deaf located on a local public school campus. Deaf students in a special day class may spend all or part of their day in this class. They may also be fully or partially included in a mainstreamed classroom. A residential school for the deaf is another option. Children can also attend a residential school for the deaf as day students if they live close enough to the school. The requirements of IDEA apply to each educational option.

IDEA guarantees certain rights to all handicapped children from ages three to twenty-one. This law recognizes the unique conditions that evolve from the various handicaps and attempts to meet these conditions. Some of the essential points of the IDEA are listed below:

- requires parent permission for initial assessment of the child

- requires a thorough, nondiscriminatory assessment of the disability

- requires that the local district hold an IEP meeting at the conclusion of the assessment for purposes of developing program and placement recommendations

- provides free and appropriate public education (FAPE) for all disabled children

- requires parent permission for placement

- gives parents access to due process through administrative hearing procedure to redress grievances concerning assessment, goals and objectives, and placement

In the case of a deaf child, the evaluators must consider the linguistic needs of the child and an interpreter must be provided, if appropriate. An appropriate nondiscriminatory evaluation of your deaf child is an essential first step in developing an appropriate IEP.

Similarly, if a child has a primary language other than English, he or she may be evaluated in the primary language. A translation of a test may not meet the cultural and linguistic needs of the child. You will need to be proactive and help guide professionals in the assessment of your child if a language other than English is spoken in your home.

If there is a disagreement between the parents and the school district, there are safeguards in place to settle disputes.

- You have a right to voice your concerns.

- Consider a compromise if the school district does not agree with you.

- You have the right to include a third party, a mediator. This is an unbiased person who will listen to both sides of the issues and make a recommendation.

- You have the right to request an independent evaluation of your child if you disagree with a particular assessment.

- You have a right to file a formal complaint and receive a state level review of the situation. This procedure is called due process and involves meetings among parents, school representatives, and a state-appointed impartial hearing officer.

- If you disagree with the outcome of the due process hearing, you may seek legal action and take the district to court.

You may request a review of all records, reports, and evaluations on your child. You can request that inaccurate records be changed. You may also ask a qualified school representative to explain your child's records to you. It is a good idea to keep copies of your child's IEPs and all other documents.

Parents may call an IEP meeting at any time. Additionally, you may request an interpreter or you may want an advocate to attend. You need to inform the district if you are going to bring an advocate. Parents must agree to the time, date, and location of the IEP meeting. If you cannot attend the meeting in person, you can participate by phone or through other forms of communication.

IFSP meetings or IEP meetings can be an emotional time for parents. Attending a meeting with a room full of experts can be intimidating. Besides hearing information that may be painful, absorbing all the new goals and objectives can be overwhelming. I have attended IEP meetings as an administrative designee, a translator, a teacher, and a parent. The most difficult role is that of a parent. Information becomes emotionally charged when it revolves around your very own child. Experts are not always sensitive communicators. Try to remain focused and don't be afraid to speak up when you are uncomfortable.

15

EDUCATIONAL PLACEMENT

very deaf or hard-of-hearing child is unique, and a child's IEP should reflect this. Placement of the child in the least restrictive environment, an essential component of the Individualized Educational Program, follows the assessment process. The intent of the least restrictive environment statement is that all children have a right to an education matched to their academic, linguistic, social, and physical needs. PL94-142 states, "The handicapped child should be educated with his nonhandicapped peers to the maximum extent possible."

There is a system of special education services available for deaf and hard-of-hearing students. One way of viewing the information is by dividing the system into levels, which are arbitrary and only used to make the information more understandable. The first level in educating deaf students is a fully included or mainstreamed classroom with or without support services. In this situation, a child may attend the neighborhood school and receive speech therapy. The second level is a fully included or mainstreamed classroom plus supplementary instructional services, which may include a full inclusion specialist or a resource pull-out program. The third level is a combination of part-time inclusion in a regular classroom and part-time special day class for the deaf. The fourth level is a full-time special day class setting with students who are all deaf and a teacher of the deaf. In levels two to four, students may be part of a day program for the deaf where the program is located on the same campus as a regular school. It also may be one special day class on a campus of a regular school. Another option is a school for the deaf that offers residential or day programs.

The definition of the term *least restrictive environment* has caused controversy in the field of deaf education. With deafness, determining what is the least restrictive environment can be problematic. Placing a deaf child in full inclusion may be considered to be following the spirit of the law because the child is being educated with hearing peers. However, there are other factors that need to be heeded. The child's social, academic, and emotional well-being are essential factors. A deaf child needs to have access to the entire learning environment.

It has been pointed out by deaf educators and members of the Deaf community that full inclusion may be the most restrictive placement for a deaf child because the child does not have the same access to information as a hearing child. Children in a school for the deaf where everyone signs fluently can fully participate and interact on every level. This refers to small group discussion, large group interactions, extracurricular activities, and social aspects of learning.

Some deaf students achieve beautifully in a setting such as a special education classroom for the deaf or a residential or day school for the deaf. Although these settings may be considered "restrictive" according to the law, they may be more consistent with a deaf child's academic and social or emotional needs. Conversely, other deaf students may be educated in the regular classroom in a full inclusion or mainstream situation with support services and achieve beautifully. There is not a single formula for educating deaf children. The intent of the law is to provide for individual needs. In the end, your family decision will carry the greatest weight in determining your child's educational placement. It is, therefore, essential that you are informed and proactive regarding your child's educational options.

16

ETIOLOGY OF HEARING LOSS

Hearing is a complicated process and much can go wrong anywhere along the auditory system. Many different conditions can cause a hearing loss in any part of the system. Hearing loss occurs on a continuum from mild to moderate and severe to profound. A person's ability to hear is as unique as his or her fingerprint. No two people have the exact same hearing loss.

The period from birth to three years is a critical period for the development of speech and language. Even a mild hearing loss can affect the course of speech and language development. Therefore, it is vital to assess and treat hearing loss in children as soon as possible.

Some of the major causes of hearing loss are hereditary factors, severe diseases that affect the cochlea and the auditory nerve, obstructions in the external auditory canal, some drugs, and high fevers.

Inner Ear Causes

The result of a hearing loss to the inner ear, or cochlea (see Figure 1), and its connecting nerves is referred to as a *sensorineural hearing loss*. It is also frequently called "nerve deafness" but this is not always an accurate description. The delicate nerve mechanisms or the thousands of tiny hair cells in the cochlea are damaged, which causes speech discrimination difficulties. Heredity, tumors, and traumatic injury are some of the causes of sensorineural types of hearing loss. Illness accompanied by high fever, especially for a prolonged period of time, meningitis, benign growths in the hearing nerve, and viral infections (mumps and measles) can also cause hearing losses. While the mother is pregnant, she may contract infections such as rubella or cytomegalovirus that can cause hearing loss in the unborn child. These infections may be so mild that the mother is not even aware of symptoms.

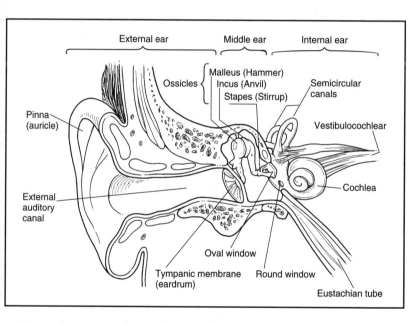

Figure 1

The ear and its anatomical structures. Note the three main portions of the ear and the associated structures.

Reprinted with permission from *Anatomy and Physiology the Easy Way* by I. Edward Alcamo. Barron's Educational Series, Inc., 1996.

Drugs and medications such as antibiotics can cause a hearing loss. Antibiotics called aminoglycosides (gentomycin, neomycin, streptomycin) and several others can be ototoxic, or harmful, to the ear depending on dosage and how long treatment lasts. These drugs destroy hair cells in the cochlea. Certain drugs taken for cancer treatment may also result in a hearing loss. Sensorineural hearing loss in general is usually permanent and requires special teaching methods such as auditory training, speech reading, and use of a manual communications system.

Outer Ear Causes

Problems with the outer ear can cause a conductive hearing loss. This simply means that something is blocking the sound from being effectively conducted to the inner ear. Malformation of the outer ear and ear canal can cause a hearing loss. The term *atresia* refers to the condition where a child is born without an ear or canal. Either one ear or both ears can be involved. Bone conduction hearing aids are helpful in these circumstances. Surgery can often correct the conductive portion of the hearing loss whether or not a sensorineural hearing loss is present. Foreign objects can cause a hearing loss, as can wax buildup. These conditions can block the auditory canal, preventing sound from entering. Children who wear hearing aids often get wax buildup in their outer ears. Periodic removal of the wax by a physician will help.

External infections of the skin lining the ear canal can cause itching, swelling, or rawness. Swimmer's ear is one such condition. These infections can become more serious and cause hearing loss if left untreated. Medication recommended by a physician can clear up these conditions.

Middle Ear Causes

Middle ear infection, called *otitis media*, is a result of the formation of buildup of fluid in the middle ear. The severity can vary, with pus forming and settling in the middle ear cavity often causing a temporary hearing loss and sometimes fluctuating hearing loss. Although this loss is usually temporary, it can become permanent without medical treatment. Middle ear infections are frequently the result of allergies, head colds, inflamed tonsils and adenoids, blocked Eustachian tubes, sore throats, or other conditions caused by viruses. Parents of infants need to take particular care to elevate a child's head when giving a bottle of milk to prevent aggravation of these conditions.

Parents of children who have a sensorineural hearing loss need to be aware of how middle ear infections will further affect their child's hearing. Compounding a sensorineural hearing loss with a middle ear infection can reduce a child's ability to hear and respond to sound. Prompt medical attention in all cases is essential.

A rupture of the eardrum can cause scarring and may even damage the tiny middle ear bones, resulting in hearing loss. Sometimes a torn eardrum will heal naturally. If the rupture is more extensive, surgery may be required. Children can also be born with damage or malformation of the middle ear. Surgical reconstruction may improve these conditions.

Hearing losses to the middle and outer ear are called *conductive hearing losses.* The degree of conductive hearing losses is variable and can usually be helped by medical or surgical attention.

Genetic Causes of Hearing Loss

One of the most important factors in the cause of significant hearing loss in children is heredity. A significant amount of both conductive and sensorineural hearing loss in children may be attributed to genetics. Scientists are researching the genetic causes of deafness and have identified some genes that are responsible. However, the number of genes responsible for hearing loss is large and the majority of genes that have been identified are genes associated with syndromes. Some of these syndromes include Waardenburgs, Ushers, Alport, Brachio-Oto-Renal, and Treacher-Collins.

Nonsyndromic hearing impairment can be identified when a child has a hearing loss and no other physical finding. This type of genetic hearing loss accounts for the majority of congenital hearing loss. Further investigation is needed to identify the genes associated with nonsyndromic deafness. The search for the genetic information is complicated for various reasons. Sometimes congenital hearing loss is caused by recessive genes and sometimes by dominant genes. As deaf individuals marry other deaf individuals and have children, the genetic puzzle becomes more difficult to trace.

It has been difficult to identify nonsyndromic hearing loss as the cause when a hearing couple with no deafness in their family histories has a deaf child. Sometimes a recessive gene is suspected but is not confirmed until the couple has a second child with a hearing loss. If each person has a recessive gene, then the couple has a 25 percent chance of having a child with a hearing loss every time they have a child. Families that have no diagnosis of why their child has a hearing loss may be suspicious of a genetic cause. Further research may prove helpful in identifying these genes.

17

HEARING TESTS

Testing infants and young children is an art. It requires diligence and patience on the part of the audiologist and the parents. An adult can get a complete audiological evaluation in about one hour. However, getting the same amount of information regarding an infant's or young child's hearing may take many visits to the audiologist. Pediatric audiologists specialize in working with children. An audiological evaluation for a young child may involve a number of tests, including Auditory Brainstem Response, Otoacoustic Emissions, Impedance, and Behavioral testing.

Auditory Brainstem Response (ABR) is the electrical response of the brain as it responds to the presence of sound. An ABR is usually done when the child is asleep. An ABR primarily tests the higher frequencies, around 2,000–4,000 hertz (Hz), but provides little information about the lower frequency spectrum. It is a test of the integrity of the auditory nerve.

Otoacoustic Emissions records frequency-specific information that is echoed back from the outer hair cells in the cochlea.

Impedance measures the movement of the eardrum and middle ear bones. It can be used to tell if there is fluid in the middle ear.

Visual Reinforcement Audiometry (VRA) is a behavioral technique used to test children under the age of two years. Children are trained to look at a visual stimulus (such as a light or moving toy) when they hear a sound. Responses are charted on the audiogram.

Play Audiometry is a behavioral technique used with children two to five years. The child drops a bead in a bucket or puts a peg in a hole when he or she hears the sound. Responses are charted on the audiogram.

Real Ear Measurement records the sound pressure at the eardrum and compares the resting measurements with the gain provided by a hearing aid. The hearing aid can then be modified to reflect the specific needs of your child.

Sound is produced by air moving back and forth quickly. A low sound is one that moves back and forth 125 times in one second, such as a foghorn. A high sound is one that moves 2,000 cycles per second, like a whistle. How fast the air molecules vibrate determines the pitch or frequency. The number of cycles per second is called *hertz* (Hz).

An audiogram is a chart of hearing. Sounds are presented across a frequency range from 250 Hz to 8,000 Hz. When the child indicates that the sound is heard, the audiologist charts the information on an audiogram. The numbers across the top show the pitch or frequency from low on the left to high on the right.

Whether high pitched or low, sounds also have another quality: intensity or loudness. The numbers from the top to the bottom of the audiogram indicate the level of intensity. A *decibel* (dB) is the unit of measurement that describes loudness or intensity. For example, 10 dB is a very quiet sound, such as a breeze blowing through leaves. On the other hand, 90 dB would refer to a very loud sound, such as a lawn mower. The loudness increases exponentially on the audiogram so that 10 dB is much more than ten times the loudness of 1 dB, and 120 dB is many thousands of times larger than 1 dB.

The frequencies or tones most important for adults who lose their hearing are 500–2,000 Hz. The frequencies most important for development of speech in children are 500–3,000 Hz. The ability to hear across these frequencies between 15 and 40 dB is critical for the development of speech and language. The area where most speech sounds occur is called the *speech range.* It is important that your child hears as much as possible in this range with his hearing aids on to develop speech and listening skills.

The quietest sound that a person can hear is called *threshold.* Someone with normal hearing has a threshold between 0 and 15 dB. Hearing loss can range from slight to profound. A slight loss ranges from 15 to 25 dB. Even a slight loss can cause a child to fail to hear some speech sounds some of the time. A mild loss is one that ranges from 25 to 40 dB of loudness. This loss can cause difficulty understanding soft speech. A child's speech may be difficult to understand because he or she may not hear some of the consonants. A moderate loss (40–65 dB), may cause a child to have difficulty understanding even normal level speech and may interfere with language development because the child fails to hear endings and small words or fails to distinguish certain vowels or consonants. A severe loss (65–90 dB) may cause a child to have difficulty understanding speech unless it is very loud or amplified. Without amplification, a child with a moderate or severe loss is unlikely to develop normal speech and language. A child with a profound loss (over 90 dB) has difficulty understanding speech even with amplification.

The degree of hearing loss can have a major impact on speech and language development (as indicated in Figure 2).

Hearing aids, speech therapy, auditory training, early language stimulation, and special educational support are recommended for all unaided hearing losses described here.

MILD LOSS (25 to 40 dB)

Receptive (what is heard)

Expressive

S P E E C H
Misses short unstressed words, syllables, and voiceless consonants (e.g., f, k, p, s, t). Vowels are heard clearly. Background noise blocks out speech sounds. May not hear faint or distant speech.

May not use voiceless consonants or unstressed syllables. Speech may be difficult to understand.

L A N G U A G E
In a quiet environment, will be able to carry on conversation and understand directions.

Vocabulary and language may be limited with word endings or whole words left out.

MODERATE LOSS (40 to 65 dB)

Receptive

Expressive

S P E E C H
Misses almost all speech at a conversational level, unless speaker is very close. Vowels are heard more easily than consonants.

Omits and distorts consonants. Difficult to understand. Special training is needed for speech development along with amplification.

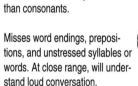

L A N G U A G E
Misses word endings, prepositions, and unstressed syllables or words. At close range, will understand loud conversation.

May have difficulty with multiple meanings and idioms. Vocabulary will be limited. Omissions include articles (a, the), conjunctions (but, or), prepositions (in, on). Word order may be mixed up.

SEVERE LOSS (65 to 90 dB)

S P E E C H

Receptive
May hear a loud voice, but not understand speech. Hears environmental sounds such as a door slamming. May be able to tell the difference between vowels, but not consonants.

Expressive
Speech and language do not develop normally without amplification and special training.

L A N G U A G E

Does not hear a conversation without amplification. Understands very little without visual and contextual clues.

Speech and language do not develop normally without amplification and special training

PROFOUND LOSS (OVER 90 DB)

S P E E C H

Receptive
Does not hear any speech. May be aware of vibration.

Expressive
Articulation, pitch, and rhythm will probably be poor. Does not develop speech naturally without amplification and special training.

L A N G U A G E

Does not understand without visual clues.

Severe language delay possible. Does not develop language without special training.

When amplification is used before one year of age, and special training is begun, the descriptions above improve a great deal depending upon degree of loss, cause of deafness, training, and motivation.

At great loss levels, visual cues are needed as well as amplification.

Figure 2

The effects of various levels of hearing loss on speech and language development.

© The SEE Center for the Advancement of Deaf Children 1987. Permission to reprint from "A Beginning ... for Parents of Deaf and Hard of Hearing Children" published by the SEE Center for the Advancement of Deaf Children, Los Alamitos, CA.

71

Usually, the more severe the loss, the more remediation and intervention is required. Another factor to consider is when the hearing loss occurred. If the loss is acquired before speech and language are established (prelinguistic), the effect on speech and language development is much greater than if the loss occured after speech and language were developed (postlinguistic).

It is important for you to understand your child's hearing loss. You must be aware of what sounds your child can hear so that you have realistic expectations for the development of speech and listening skills. Keep a file at home of all the records of hearing testing. Make sure that all hearing tests and audiologist reports are forwarded to your child's teacher.

18

HEARING AIDS

Selecting the most appropriate amplification for your child will be one of the most important decisions that you make. You will have to work with your audiologist to determine the best hearing aid. The decision is often difficult with a young child because the information that you have in the beginning may be minimal. Therefore, the audiologist may suggest trying different hearing aids or different settings on the hearing aid. Your observations of your child's response to sound (which sounds seem not to be heard and which sounds seem to be too loud or uncomfortable) should be reported to the audiologist to help determine which aid or setting is best.

A hearing aid is a battery-powered electronic device that makes sound louder and takes the sound directly to the ear. It has three main parts: the *microphone* picks up the sound from the environment; the *amplifier* changes the sound into an electric signal and makes the sound louder; and the *receiver* changes the amplified signal back to sound waves that enter the ear.

An ear mold is worn in the opening of the outer ear and is attached to the hearing aid. It is made of plastic material and is custom fit by the hearing aid dealer to each child's ear. With very young children who are growing rapidly, new ear molds may have to be made every few months to fit the changing ear. You will generally know when you need a new mold because you will hear feedback—a whistling sound that comes from the hearing aid. Sometimes you will get feedback from a new ear mold, which may indicate that it does not fit properly. You can take it back to the dealer immediately for a free replacement. There are different materials for making ear molds. If one material seems to irritate your child, then ask for the mold to be made of an alternative material.

Here are some terms that you will hear regarding your child's hearing aids:

Gain is a word that refers to the decibel amount of amplification. For example, 30 dB of gain refers to making the sound louder by 30 decibels.

Maximum power output (MPO) refers to the loudest sound that a hearing aid is set to produce. This protects your child from getting sounds that would be loud enough to hurt him or her.

Volume control is generally a wheel that makes the sounds louder as they come out of the hearing aid. The audiologist will recommend a volume setting that will be appropriate for your child. If your child does not respond at that setting, the audiologist may recommend a higher setting. If you get feedback at the recommended setting and have to turn the hearing aid to a lower setting to stop the feedback, then it may be time to get a new ear mold. This must be done immediately because turning the volume down to reduce feedback can make the hearing aid no better than a plug in the ear.

The battery is what gives the hearing aid power and it is very important for you to make sure that you are using the recommended type and size of battery for the hearing aid.

You may use a battery tester to make sure the battery is working.

Standard or analog hearing aids are often recommended for children. These aids have internal settings that can be changed to generally follow the slope of your child's audiogram. For example, if your child hears more in the low frequencies than in the high frequencies, the aid can be adjusted to cut out low sounds and increase amplification in the high sounds. It may be necessary to try different hearing aids to see which aid best suits your child. Sometimes the audiologist will loan hearing aids for a trial period to help determine which aids are most appropriate.

The newest type of hearing aid is a digitally programmable hearing aid. The advantage of these aids is that they can be programmed in a more specific way. They can be set to the very specific amplification characteristics of your child. It is a simple matter to reprogram the aids as the audiologist gets more information about what your child is hearing. These aids tend to be more expensive than standard aids because they are more flexible and can be programmed by a computer. However, they may be the best choice because changing the settings is cheaper than buying new hearing aids. Parents are sometimes asked to buy new hearing aids when the audiologist gets more information about the child's hearing and changes the recommendation. The audiologist will help you determine which kind of hearing aids are best for your child.

There are several types of hearing aids:

In the ear or in the canal hearing aids are generally aids that do not provide a lot of gain. They are generally worn by adults who have lost some hearing and are considered hard of hearing.

Behind the ear (BTE) hearing aids are small hearing aids that are worn behind the ear. Plastic tubing connects the ear mold to the aid. These aids are now available for most children and can provide a high gain. Because BTEs are worn behind each ear, they help children learn to localize or find the sound source.

Body aids look like a small box and are worn in a vest on the chest. A cord attaches the aid to the ear mold. The microphone is at the chest and, therefore, it is difficult for children to localize sound wearing this type of aid. These aids used to be recommended for children who needed high gain hearing aids. However, behind the ear hearing aids can now provide the same amount of gain and localization ability.

Bone conduction hearing aids consist of a headband and a vibrator worn against the skull behind the ear. The sound travels through the bone to the cochlea and bypasses the outer and middle ear. These aids are beneficial for children with atresia or with middle ear malfunction. Conductive losses respond well to hearing aids because the only factor you are dealing with is intensity. There is no deterioration of hair cells as in sensorineural losses.

19

USING AMPLIFICATION

Consistent and appropriate amplification is absolutely essential for developing your child's speech and listening skills. Consistent means that your child wears his or her hearing aids every minute of the day. Hearing children have heard even before they were born. If your child only wears the hearing aids two hours a day, it would take many years to get the same amount of listening time as a hearing child would get in one year.

Your child does not hear exactly what a person with normal hearing hears, even with optimal amplification. He or she needs to learn to interpret the auditory information received. The sound will be different for each child. Each audiogram is different, with each child hearing some speech sounds better than others. Some speech sounds may be impossible for your child to hear.

Purchasing two hearing aids is a major investment for most families. You want to be sure that you get a hearing aid that has a wide range of flexibility. This means that the internal settings can be changed and reset to fit your child's hearing loss as you get more information about what your child is hearing.

Every child's hearing loss is different and the aid that best fits one child will not work for another. Some hearing aids are very powerful and amplify sounds to the maximum. However, just making the sounds louder is not always the answer. It is important to hear as many speech sounds as possible because that helps your child decipher the speech, but some sounds may actually be too loud for your child's comfort. The intelligibility or clarity of the speech that your child is hearing is most important.

Once you have purchased your child's hearing aids, it is then your responsibility to check the aids daily and to keep them in working order. You can listen to your child's aid with a hearing aid stethoscope. With daily listening checks, you are likely to notice when the aid is not functioning properly. And the problem can then be fixed promptly. If you feel there is a problem, you must take the aid to the hearing aid dealer to have it tested. Hearing aid molds must fit well so that you can keep your child's aids at the recommended setting. Then you must make sure that your child wears his or her hearing aids full time. Listening and speech skills cannot develop without many hours of practice.

Your audiologist or a trained teacher of the deaf can explain what your child is hearing. Audiological assessment includes testing without hearing aids. This is called unaided testing. Audiologists use this information to determine what hearing aids are most appropriate for your child and what settings are optimal. After your child has worn hearing aids for awhile, the audiologist will want to test your child to find out what your child is hearing with his or her hearing aids. This is called *aided level testing*. This information is used to plan an auditory program for your child. Have your audiologist explain your child's audiogram and what sounds your child can hear with the hearing aids on. Learning to listen takes time. It is not like putting on a pair of glasses and being able to see clearly.

The audiogram in Figure 3 shows the approximate frequency and intensity of some vowels and consonants. The

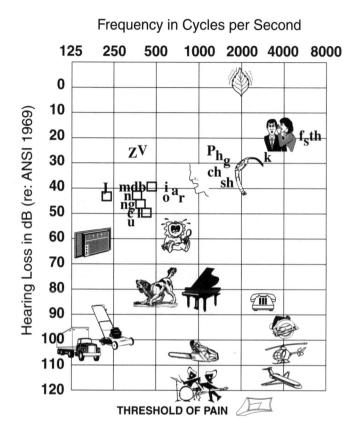

Figure 3
Frequency spectrum of familiar sounds.

Reprinted with permission from *Hearing in Children*, 3rd ed., by Jerry L. Northern and Marion P. Downs. Williams & Wilkins, 1991.

point at which your child can just barely hear a sound is called the *auditory threshold*. The sounds are easier to hear if they are above threshold. Chart your child's aided response (threshold) on this audiogram. If your child's aided responses are above the vowels and consonants on the audiogram, then your child should be able to detect them. If the levels are below the vowels or consonants, then your child will not be able to hear them.

However, it is important to remember that just because your child is able to detect the sounds does not mean he or she will be able to understand them. The most complicated sounds that your child will be asked to understand and discriminate are speech sounds. These are also the most significant sounds in his or her environment. Learning to decipher speech is a complex process. Your child must listen to a series of individual sounds that are combined to make words and sentences. Then the brain must be able to make sense of this rapid sequencing of sounds. Your child must learn a series of skills to help him or her understand what you are saying. First, your child must learn to listen for speech even if there is competing noise. Next, he or she must learn to hear differences in individual speech sounds and combinations of sounds. The word "up" sounds different from the word "down." Later, your child may be able to tell the difference between the words "mad" and "sad." He or she must then learn how to blend individual sounds into words and remember the sequence of the sounds in order to understand what is said and to reproduce the words.

The complexities of deciphering speech include the integration of more than one system. A poignant example comes to mind. One student, Cathy, had an audiogram that indicated that she could detect most of the speech sounds above threshold. Given this information, it appeared that this child would be a successful oral child. Interestingly, this was not the case. Cathy did not start using her voice until she began using sign language. Though she could hear these sounds, the speech did not make any sense until she had the help of a visual system. As a teenager, she was able to reflect and articulate on this situation herself. She was able to perceive speech but was not always able to grasp the essence of the message. The signs gave meaning to the sounds. Many factors go into hearing, and you can never truly predict a child's ability to comprehend speech based on the audiogram alone.

You also need to provide an appropriate environment for listening and speech development. Make sure that your child is in a quiet environment. Your child needs to hear your voice. Competing background noise will make it difficult for your child to discriminate speech sounds. Noises from the radio and television are obviously distracting. However, other low humming noises that you and I automatically ignore can be a problem for a child wearing hearing aids. Listen to the noises in your home through your child's hearing aid and you will see how they are amplified. Some noises to be aware of are heaters, dishwashers, refrigerators, or traffic sounds. Noisy restaurants are particularly difficult places in which to have conversations if there is background noise, uncarpeted floors, and acoustically untreated ceilings.

Learning to listen takes a great deal of concentration on the part of the child. Straining to listen to very quiet sounds can be exhausting. You can help your child by being aware of the effect that distance has on the loudness of the sounds. When you are closer to your child, he or she will be able to hear you better. If you want your child to really listen to your speech and attend to the sounds, you should be within a distance of three feet.

20

~~~~~~

PRACTICAL TIPS

After your child is fitted with hearing aids, the first challenge you will face is getting the molds in the ear and the hearing aid on before your child has grabbed them. You may want a partner to help you with this the first time. Choose someone who has a relationship with your child and can hold his or her attention. A few items may also help you to complete this task successfully. High chairs are good because they keep your child reasonably still and have trays that can hold a favorite toy or cookie to entertain your child while you acquaint yourself with the hearing aids and how to get them on your child. Furthermore, most babies and toddlers have had positive experiences with high chairs and will not object when placed in one.

After your child is secure in the high chair, engage his or her attention in a toy. A good choice is one that makes a noise that can be heard with the hearing aids on. Soft toys such as rubber ducks that squeak when pressed are good choices for babies, as are rattles, and toys with bells inside. Consider your child's developmental stage as well as favorite toys. Play with the toy in front of the child, with an engaging expression. Smile, talk, sign, clap, laugh, and model how you want your child to play with the toy. After your child reaches for it and is playing with the toy independently, begin your task. Start by inserting the mold into the ear. A lubricant recommended by your audiologist may help make the mold slide in more easily. Make sure that the mold is all the way in and secure. Place the tube and hearing aid over and behind the ear and turn it on. If your child begins to reach for the hearing aid, grasp his or her hands gently into your own and clap. Sing and play patty-cake or another finger game or a song such as "This Little Piggy" or "Eensie Weensie Spider," anything that keeps little hands away from the hearing aids.

My son loved having his belly tickled. We used this to our advantage when he began to wear hearing aids. As soon as his hearing aids were in place, secure and functioning, we would tickle his belly. He began to lift his shirt when he saw us with his hearing aids in hand. Later, when he wanted his hearing aids, he would communicate his wish by lifting his shirt! My daughter loved puzzles. When it came time to put on her hearing aids, I would get out her favorite puzzle and sit with her in front of me between my legs. The puzzle kept her hands busy and it took her several minutes to put one together. This was helpful to me in the beginning as I was inexperienced with hearing aids. Trying to get a busy toddler to stay still long enough to put hearing aids on was a challenge.

After the hearing aids are in place, play with your child. Sing a song, make animal sounds, or play with a pleasant-sounding toy. Before long, hearing aids will become part of your routine of getting dressed and your child will be able to do it alone. The messages your child receives now about the hearing aids will be important in the development of his or her self-esteem. Make this a positive and enjoyable time with your child.

It is a good practice to secure your child's hearing aids, especially as a baby and toddler. Eyeglass holders work beautifully. Slip the loops from the eyeglass holder over the tubing between the mold and the hearing aid. You will need to detach the hearing aid from the mold. Secure the holder to the back of your child's clothing with a safety pin or clip. Clips are recommended as they won't hurt your child if they become unhooked. Hearing aid dealers have special clips designed for this purpose. If your child removes the hearing aids, they will dangle behind him or her if they are secured with a pin or clip. Make sure you put your child's hearing aids back on immediately. This will prevent him or her from playing with the aids, molds, and tubing. If your child puts the hearing aid into his or her mouth, it could present a serious choking hazard. You must also make sure that your child is not able to open the battery case. Batteries, if swallowed, can be toxic. Babies and toddlers need to be supervised while wearing hearing aids.

Prepare yourself for the inevitable. It takes many years for a child to understand the importance of keeping hearing aids on and the expense that goes with it. You may have your aids flushed down the toilet, fed to the dog, or pitched from a car window, even if you are vigilant. Get insurance for the hearing aid either by putting it on your homeowner's policy or by getting a separate policy available through hearing aid dealers. Purchase or sign the warranty that comes with your hearing aids. I laugh when my friends become upset over a missing hair bow or sock. Whenever I am separated from my children even for a few minutes, I always check to see if the hearing aids are intact.

Secure a special place for hearing aids and begin training your child to put the hearing aids in this place every time the aids are removed. Bathrooms are not a good place because of the moisture. A small dish on the dresser in your child's room is recommended. When traveling, put the hearing aids in an airtight plastic container. It is a good idea to use tissue or paper towel to protect the hearing aids in case the container is dropped.

I don't insist that my young children wear the hearing aids in the car, especially for long car rides. Over-the-shoulder seat belts and car seats cause lots of feedback. Furthermore, while driving, I cannot attend to my children and so hearing aids end up on the floor, behind car seats, or possibly being swallowed. If one of the children falls asleep, then the aid can feedback and this can also become uncomfortable. As the children take more responsibility for their hearing aids, they will wear them in the car more often.

Our family has developed a system of communication in the car that suits our needs. When possible, we sign. However, with one child in front and one in back, this becomes problematic. I have placed 3×5 cards on a ring with illustrations and words of the places we frequent: the park, the store, the doctor's office, the gas station, Grandma's house, and school. Some of the cards also contain messages: water, juice, cracker. When I want to tell the kids where we are going, I simply flip to the appropriate card.

I developed this system shortly after my daughter was diagnosed at age two. She became increasingly difficult to put in the car. I soon realized that she didn't know if she was going to the doctor's office or the park to play. She enjoyed holding the cards, pondering each carefully. Later, after much practice associating the card with the location, Meghan created her own card. Her first locator card was her very own representation of McDonald's. Now she not only draws illustrations for cards, she labels them with words.

Although cars, beds, bathtubs, and swimming pools may be exceptions, hearing aids should be worn as much as possible in every situation. This is important for your child's speech and language development. However, you can also gain essential clues from observing your child as he or she maneuvers through the world of sound. Observe what sounds your child reacts to with the hearing aids on. Does he or she hear the phone? the doorbell? Which toys can be heard? What animal sounds? a bird squawking, a dog barking? Does your child turn when his or her name is called? What words does he or she respond to? what speech sounds? Keep a log of these sounds and the reactions they elicit in your child. Share this information with your audiologist and teacher. If your child is frightened by a particular sound or does not show response to sounds, it may mean you need a trip back to the audiologist to adjust the hearing aid or find an explanation. If your child enjoys a particular sound, it may trigger a teaching opportunity.

Shortly after my daughter got her hearing aids, we took a family trip to a favorite park. To get to the picnic area, we had to cross a bridge that had a small river running under it. As we got closer to the bridge, Meghan became increasingly apprehensive. By the time we reached the bridge, she was panicked. The sound of the rushing water under the bridge was too loud with her hearing aids set as they had been to amplify high sounds. After further observation and testing, we soon learned that Meghan has a reverse curve hearing loss. Meghan has more hearing in the high frequencies than in the low frequencies.

Parents, through observation, can provide audiologists, doctors, and teachers with valuable information. Gather all the clues you can regarding your child's hearing and share the information with the professionals involved in his or her care.

21

COCHLEAR IMPLANTS

A *cochlear implant* is a device designed to allow a deaf person to perceive sound. It has two separate components. The first is a surgically implanted electrode array. The second is a speech processor worn externally. The cochlear implant functions when sound is picked up by the microphone and sent to the speech processor. The processor selects the important features of speech. Adults have received multichannel electrode implants since 1984. Single electrode implants have been in use since 1964. However, this technology was not approved for children until 1990.

The cochlear implant works differently than hearing aids. A hearing aid is an external device that makes sounds louder. Sometimes these louder sounds will be perceived by the child and other times the sounds will not be loud enough for the child to hear them. The cochlear implant is a surgically implanted device that directly stimulates the auditory nerve fibers in the cochlea. The multiple electrode channels of the implant stimulate different parts of the cochlea. Therefore, the child is able to perceive sounds across the speech range from low to high. The result is that children are often able to hear high frequency consonants that they would never be able to hear with a hearing aid on. This ability to hear across the speech range and hear all the speech sounds is important in developing and understanding speech.

Generally, cochlear implants are recommended for profoundly deaf individuals who receive little or no benefit from their hearing aids. Maximum benefits occur when the person has heard before and is implanted soon after losing his or her hearing. These individuals can easily learn to interpret the new sounds from the implant as speech. For children who are born deaf, the greatest benefits occur when the child is implanted at a young age. These children have had a shorter period of auditory deprivation and the brain is more plastic. Therefore, many children are being considered for an implant at an early age. The FDA approves cochlear implants for children as young as eighteen months.

An evaluation is completed by a multidisciplinary team to decide whether the child is a candidate for an implant. The team includes the audiologist, a speech therapist, the deaf educator who works with the child at home or in the classroom, a psychologist, and an otologist. It is important that the candidate and/or parents have realistic expectations about what an implant will accomplish. It is not a cure for deafness. Every child's response is different. The family must understand that the ability to interpret speech sounds through the implant may take several years. There is no guarantee that the child will develop the perfect speech that hearing parents long for.

The family must be highly motivated and willing to participate in the child's listening training program. This means keeping many speech and audiology appointments. Parents must also keep a positive attitude about the implant and be willing to wait to see the results without getting discouraged. They must be willing and able to keep the equipment working and to encourage the child to use the device consistently.

Audiological assessment of the child prior to the implant is crucial in making the decision. It is important that the child have a trial period wearing hearing aids. The aids must be worn consistently at home and school. The child should also be enrolled in a program to train speech and listening. The audiologist and the otologist want to be sure that the lack of response to sound is due to the hearing loss, not to inconsistent amplification and lack of training.

There are a few contraindications for an implant. These include medical problems such as damage to the auditory nerve, absence of a cochlea, ossification of the cochlea, or other diseases in the ear. If the child is getting good benefit from conventional hearing aids and the implant would not improve his or her ability to hear speech, the implant is not needed. With older children, the team must be sure that the child really wants the implant and is not doing it to please his or her parents. The family must have realistic expectations and not expect a cure. Children with other disabilities and in educational settings that are entirely manual may not be candidates for the implant.

Candidates for cochlear implants can come from both total communication settings as well as auditory/oral settings. The most important factor for success is that the program includes speech and listening training. If the child is in a total communication program, some time each day needs to be spent practicing the listening and speech skills without the signs.

The idea of surgery is frightening for the parents of many deaf children. The implant involves major surgery with risks such as facial paralysis, dizziness, facial pain, and ringing in the ears. It is difficult for parents to face this decision because they must decide when the child is young. They cannot wait until the child is old enough to be part of the decision-making process.

This decision is also made more difficult because many Deaf adults feel that the surgery is not necessary because deafness is not a disease to be cured. They feel that they are whole and complete people who are a cultural and linguistic minority that is unique. Deaf children should not be subjected to a surgery to make them more like hearing people. This is an affront to a child's emotional and social well-being. Changing a deaf child's state of being is comparable to changing the color of one's skin.

After considering the data, facts, and subjective input from differing opinions, you will want to consider your own value system. Understanding the technical information and evaluating advice is challenging. However, sifting through your own thoughts and feelings may be even more challenging. Do not make a decision for or against a cochlear implant for your child if you are feeling pressured, angry, or bitter. If you make this decision with tranquility in your soul, you will have a mechanism to cope with whatever challenges your decision brings.

22

CHOICES AND DECISIONS

Your deaf or hard-of-hearing child has a need and desire to share and receive information. Your child's deafness does not affect his or her incredible impulse to communicate. Frustration and anxiety mount when this natural impulse is denied. Although the deafness affects hearing and speech, the impulse to communicate remains strong.

One of the first decisions you will be faced with is choosing a communication method for your child. The foremost issue you must address is whether or not you will use sign language with your child. Everyone in the field of deaf education has very strong feelings about communication methods. These feelings are often accompanied by a missionary zeal. Parents can be accosted by perfect strangers who tell you that what you are doing is wrong, whether you are using signs with your child or not. This may be confusing for some parents because the experts disagree on what is the best method for teaching a deaf or hard-of-hearing child.

Your decision should be based on what is the best approach for your family and your child. Carefully evaluate the needs of your child, keeping focused on the relationship that you want to develop. Which method of communication will include your whole family?

Sign Language and Sign Language Systems

Sign language and sign language systems are used for both communication and as a way to teach English. Following are definitions of the types of sign language used in the United States. It is important to understand the different choices (as indicated in Figure 4) when evaluating any program for your child.

American Sign Language

American Sign Language (ASL) is used by Deaf adults and children to communicate in the United States and Canada. It is a true language with its own grammar and its own social linguistic properties. The grammar and word order is different from English. Concepts are signed rather than English words. English is translated into ASL as it would be into any spoken language. One ASL sign may be used for many English words and vice versa.

Manually Coded English Systems

Seeing Essential English (SEE I), Signing Exact English (SEE 2), and Conceptually Accurate Signed English (CASE) are sign systems. They differ from ASL in that they are not true languages. The intention of these systems is to present a clear, manual representation of grammatically correct English. Some of the signs are the same as ASL signs. Others have an initialized handshape. Typically, these systems have one sign to represent an English word rather than a concept. New signs are made up for English words that have no signs. The use of word endings parallels English. SEE 2 is the most widely used manually coded English system.

Pigeon Sign English

Pigeon Sign English (PSE) combines some signs and concepts of ASL with English word order. Few endings are used. PSE does not provide a language model for either ASL or English.

G R A M M A R	SIGNING EXACT ENGLISH (SEE)	PIGEON SIGN ENGLISH (PSE)	AMERICAN SIGN LANGUAGE (ASL)
	English word order. Every word has a sign. Signs have been created for all word endings, prefixes, and suffixes.	English word order. May use a few endings, but usually drops them and may omit entire words, e.g., "He go school."	Does not follow English word order. Does not sign English word endings (-s, -ed, etc.)

V O C A B U L A R Y	SIGNING EXACT ENGLISH (SEE)	PIGEON SIGN ENGLISH (PSE)	AMERICAN SIGN LANGUAGE (ASL)
	Follows English vocabulary. E.g., "toys" would be signed "toy + s" and the basic sign for "beauty" is made with "p" for "pretty," "l" for "lovely," with "-ful" for "beautiful," etc.	Uses same vocabulary as ASL; may add a few SEE signs.	Different vocabulary from English; e.g., "toys" might be "play things" or "doll, ball, etc." One sign may be used, with different intensity, for "pretty, lovely, beautiful," etc.

E N D I N G S	SIGNING EXACT ENGLISH (SEE)	PIGEON SIGN ENGLISH (PSE)	AMERICAN SIGN LANGUAGE (ASL)
	Uses signs for all endings (e.g., -s, -ed, -ing, -ly, -ment, -tion, etc.)	May use a few endings (-ing, -ness) but drops most.	Does not use word endings of English. Shows tense with time words (yesterday, tomorrow, etc.)

WRITTEN AS THE SENTENCE/CONCEPT WOULD BE SIGNED IN THAT MODE:

E X A M P L E	SEE	PSE	ASL
	We are leaving as soon as the movie is over.	We leave quick movie finish.	Movie finish, zoom two-of-us.

Figure 4

Differences in sign systems.

The following list will help you understand the communication choices available and understand the terms that you will be hearing.

Aural/Oral Choices

Auditory Verbal, Auditory, Auditory Oral, and Verbotonal

Aural and oral terms refer to methods that rely on auditory training and speech training to develop oral language. Aural refers to hearing and oral refers to speech. The use of sign language is discouraged. Children are encouraged to use their residual hearing (hearing that is available to the child with hearing aids) to learn speech and language. Often you will see therapists or teachers talk to the child behind the child's back or while covering their mouth. Oral methods also include training in speech reading or lipreading.

Cued Speech

Cued speech is an oral method that uses hand cues around the mouth to tell the child what sounds are being made. For example, three cues might be cued for the word mouth (/m/ou/th/). The cues do not denote any concepts or words but strictly sounds. This method may not be available in your area.

Pros for Oral/Aural Approaches

- Emphasis is on developing speech so that the child can function in a hearing world.

- Use of residual hearing and the latest technology available is encouraged.

- Parents do not have to change their way of communication.

Cons for Oral/Aural Approaches

- Limited exposure to other deaf children and adults.

- Deafness is seen as a handicapping condition, a medical problem to be fixed with technology.

- Language learning may be compromised because children miss valuable information using listening alone.

Sign Language Options

Bilingual/Bicultural

    American Sign Language (ASL) is used for communication. Children are taught in ASL to provide a strong language foundation. Following the theories of bilingual/bicultural education with hearing children, a complete first language is established in ASL. English is acquired through print. The strong skills in language and communication facilitate the acquisition of English as a second language. The deaf child has the added bonus of access to two cultures and two languages.

Pros for Bilingual /Bicultural

- Hearing families are welcomed and have access to the Deaf community, culture, and language. Children and parents have access to Deaf role models.

- Self-esteem of the Deaf child is of primary consideration. Deafness is not seen as a handicapping condition but as a cultural/linguistic difference that deserves respect.

- ASL establishes a strong primary language system and English is supported through print.

Cons for Bilingual/Bicultural

- ASL is a priority in the classroom. However, there is no continual access to spoken English. Speech and listening are practiced on an individual basis.

- Hearing parents may have a difficult time becoming fluent ASL signers and as a result are not good ASL role models for their children.

- "Fix-it" technologies such as cochlear implants are negatively viewed.

Total Communication

Total communication generally refers to an educational philosophy that supports any method including sign language, gestures, written language, and aural/oral methods to teach language to deaf children. The term was coined in the early 1970s by Roy Holcomb. It has become a term that means different things to different people. The sign systems that are used vary from place to place, although generally Pigeon Sign English or a Manually Coded English system is used. In most schools that call themselves total communication programs, students, teachers, and parents use both signed English and spoken English simultaneously.

Pros for Total Communication

- Hearing parents are able to transmit their native language, English, through the use of signs to their child. It may be easier to learn a sign system because signs match spoken English words.

- Information is available to children in both sign and speech. Parents are encouraged to take advantage of all the technology available.

- Children have the tools necessary to participate in both the hearing and deaf cultures. Manually Coded English is learned first and helps children learn to read English.

Cons for Total Communication

- The Deaf community views Manually Coded English as an interference on ASL, the language of the Deaf.

- Many programs lack consistency in sign use. Teachers may have a range of skill level from beginning to fluent. Different systems may also be used in classes within the same school.

- It is difficult to place equal emphasis simultaneously on both signs and speech. It is difficult to sign everything you say. Many important words may be omitted.

Every parent of every deaf or hard-of-hearing child grapples with the choices and decisions revolving around methods. After you have gathered information, you will have taken your first steps in making your decision. Remain focused on your child as an individual. Learn from your child. Your child is your best guide. By observing your child's steps in both sign and speech, your direction will become clearer. Some of the bumps in your path may include experts who dictate what you must do and your own anxieties and insecurities revolving around your desire to have your child talk.

23

OTHER FACTORS
TO CONSIDER

There are many things that you can do to help you decide on an appropriate educational program for your child. Read books about different choices. Talk to people who advocate different choices. Try signing with your child and evaluate how your child responds to the signs. Drop the signs and use listening and speech alone and evaluate how your child responds. Some children love the signs and immediately respond by signing back; others don't pay much attention and prefer speech.

Numerous factors will influence your decision. The degree of hearing loss, your child's ability to use residual hearing to learn English, and your child's ability to use speech and to process any language will be factors that affect your decision. Your willingness and ability to learn sign language, your child's preferred learning style, and the type of educational programs available to you in your area will also play important roles in deciding on a communication system. It is also important to consider when the hearing loss occurred. Children who lose their hearing before language is established (prelingually deaf) must develop a complete language system. Children who are postlingually deaf already have a language system established and must learn to adapt to their loss. Every child's situation and hearing loss are unique and decisions must be made on an individual basis.

Visit the educational programs that are available. Your primary focus will be the communication methodology they use. Do they use sign language or not? What sign system are they using? Other factors you want to observe include: the overall quality of the program, the convenience of the program, the ability to provide experiences with hearing children if that is important to you, educational opportunities for parents, a supportive community for your family, a peer group for your child where he or she can develop friendships, deaf role models, and the flexibility of the program to meet your needs as a family.

Some parents feel very strongly about a particular method or sign system and will relocate to find a program that follows that method of teaching or sign system. However, many parents are not able to move their whole family to meet the needs of one child. You may have to design a program that fits your circumstances. If you have an oral-only choice, you may then decide to sign with your child at home even though in school they are not using signs. Conversely, if your best choice is a sign program that does not offer enough practice in developing speech and listening, you may supplement with private speech and listening therapy.

As the parent, you have to make communication and educational decisions. Whatever decision you make, you must realize that the language learning that takes place in the home cannot be duplicated in school later. The first five years of life are a critical time for developing language. As the parent, you are the most important player and will have the most influence on your child's development. You must actively participate in your child's language learning. It is through parent-child interactions that hearing children develop mastery of English. The same is true for deaf and hard-of-hearing children.

You cannot afford to sit back and let a teacher or an audiologist make the decisions for you. You need to educate yourself to navigate through the maze of choices and decisions that you must face. You must understand the complex learning that takes place when children learn English. It seems easy and natural when the children can hear. However, deafness can get in the way of developing mastery of English. If this happens, your child is at a great disadvantage in the world. Academic success is based on your child's ability to manipulate the English language through speech, signing, reading, and writing.

As a parent, you must learn what you can do to insure that your child can understand, read, and express himself or herself fluently in English through sign and/or speech and writing. Each communication method has had both successes and failures. Remember to focus on the method that will help your child develop mastery of the English language. You must decide which method will give you the tools to help your child develop into a successful learner of English.

Whether you use ASL, a signed English system, or an auditory/oral approach, your child must master all aspects of the English language to be successful.

24

SPEECH AND LANGUAGE

Language is at the true core of what makes us uniquely human. It is what brings us together and separates us as nothing else. Language is the glue that allows us to establish and maintain our relationships. It is the way in which we transmit our most intimate thoughts and feelings. It is what we use to love and discipline our children. Without a common language, our thoughts, feelings, and opinions are misinterpreted or lost. A place without words to reach the very people we want to touch is indeed very lonely.

Deaf educators often talk about speech and language very differently. Language enables people to express their thoughts and feelings, solve personal problems, and reach beyond their present circumstances. Language may be the most important tool for receiving information and knowledge. Speech, contrastingly, is one way of expressing language. It is the way that the majority of people express their thoughts and feelings. However, there are other ways of expressing language that most people have never thought about. Using sign language is a way that many deaf people around the world communicate and express language. Writing is another way of expressing language that is used extensively. New technologies such as the Internet have given us new ways to use language creatively and globally. It is essential that you constantly reflect on the difference between speech and language and distinguish between the two.

A language delay is far more serious than a speech delay. Parents need to understand the devastating effects on a child's development when language learning is delayed. Learning, reading, and academic skills are not hindered by a speech delay. However, a language delay can significantly interrupt the acquisition of reading and writing skills and have a profound effect on a child's academic future. Therefore, it is logical that you focus on language acquisition especially during a child's first years of life. The way your child expresses language is not as important as the fact that he or she is developing a complete language system. A deaf child may be developing language through the use of signs rapidly. However, speech development may be progressing at a slower pace.

Having understandable speech will always help your child navigate in a hearing world. It will make your child's life easier to be able to use oral language to communicate with the hearing people he or she meets. It is important to remember that speech skills can be developed. Some people are very talented and natural at picking up these skills just as some people are talented at sports or at the piano. Practice also plays an important role in developing speech and listening skills. However, someone without natural talent could practice for hours and hours at the piano or at a sport without becoming a virtuoso or a sports star. Your child is an individual with special talents and multiple abilities. Treat him or her as an individual.

Parents and society often are concerned with the child's ability to speak. Parents are often told that it is a hearing world and that their children must learn to adapt to it. Parents become very concerned with therapy and drills to "correct" their child's speech. Do not fall into the trap where you judge your child's success by his or her ability to use speech. Speech or the sound of one's voice has little or nothing to do with language ability or higher thinking skills. Many Deaf adults have told us that repetitious drills in speech and listening as a child took the place of other more important learning. In other words, they spent a lot of time working on the sound of their voice and missed important concept development in academic areas.

Hearing parents are often shocked when their deaf or hard-of-hearing child has trouble functioning in a normal academic environment. However, the school, the classroom, or the teacher cannot substitute for the early language learning that is the basis for all later learning. Many times, parents limit interactions to simple directions when they are speaking to their deaf child. The deaf child is not asked about his or her opinions or feelings. The deaf child is not overhearing conversations or asked to comment on experiences and activities. The deaf child's language repertoire is limited in these circumstances. It is hardly a surprise that deaf children with limited language suffer in cognitively demanding situations. As mentioned previously, parents are their child's first teachers and must make every effort to impart a strong language foundation to their deaf or hard-of-hearing child.

Higher learning requires that children have established a strong language foundation. Around third or fourth grade, learning in the American educational system changes from hands-on, visual, and manipulative-based instruction. Suddenly, children are asked to read independently and respond to literature in abstract ways. They are required to compare and contrast, identify elements of a story, make inferences, and draw conclusions. Children who do not have a comprehensive language foundation are at a great disad-

Meghan's physical talents in soccer feed her self-esteem and connect her with hearing children in a positive way.

vantage in the classroom because the vital role of language development in nurturing intellectual development has been ignored. An unfortunate consequence is the loss of self-esteem and the deep sense of failure that further prevents deaf students from becoming successful academically.

There are many deaf adults and children who do not have perfect speech but do have good English language skills. These deaf people function competently in the workplace as a result of their good English language skills. They also function at high levels in their environments, whether at school or work or in social situations. The lack of speech does not get in the way of high-level functioning but can present a challenge in interacting with hearing people. Good

English language skills, writing, and reading can compensate for a speech deficit.

Most parents want both high-level speech and high-level language for their children. For many parents, the concern with speech is actually concern for their child's language development because they don't understand the difference between speech and language. The danger is when the focus on speech takes precedence over learning language during the preschool years. Remember, you can get speech therapy at any age to help improve speech production. If you miss the critical period for learning language, the intricacies of English may always be a mystery.

Everyone has dreams for their child. This can be wonderful if your child has the same dreams as you do. However, many times, the child has different dreams, abilities, and talents than parents hope for. Look at your child as an individual and see what his or her abilities, talents, and dreams are. Speech may be one of your child's strengths or it may not. Look at your child's assets, not deficits.

25

STRATEGIES FOR COMMUNICATION

Your deaf or hard-of-hearing child has awarded you new learning experiences. Consider the deafness as a bridge to new learning and not a barrier to communication. The new dynamics in your family can be exciting and rewarding. Communicating with comfort and ease in and outside your home is emotionally and socially healthy for you and your deaf child. Active participation and communication in the home and community will satisfy your deaf child's hunger for communication and information.

Following is a list of strategies to incorporate into your communication system in your home. Consistent use of these strategies will give your child positive messages about communication.

- Sign with your child. Using sign language is one place where deaf and hearing family members can meet. It will make communication easier for your child, although it may be difficult for the parent.

- Keep eye contact while your child is communicating.

- Wait a second or so before responding to your child. This helps to keep a good conversational pace.

- Take turns when talking—make a rule in family conversations that one person talks/signs at a time.

- Be patient as your child communicates. Focus on the message.

- Let your child's words be his or her own. Avoid filling in or speaking your child's thoughts or ideas.

- Allow your child to complete his or her thoughts without interrupting.

- After your child communicates, reply slowly using some of the same words.

- Devote time to communicating with your child in an easy and relaxed manner. When you talk to your deaf child, you need to give him or her your full attention. You cannot do the dishes and talk as you can with a hearing child.

- Put aside a special time every week or every day when you can give your deaf child your undivided attention and answer questions and share all the things that have happened that day or that week. For example, Grandma may have called and told you some information about her health. This is information that a hearing child would easily pick up.

- Show your child that you value and respect him or her and enjoy time together. Find activities and interests that you share with your deaf child and develop these interests together. These activities could be sports, hobbies, Girl Scouts, or crafts.

- Make sure that your child knows the names of people who are part of your life—family members and friends. It is important that you explain how these people are related to your child. Make a book of pictures of family members with names and name signs.

Meghan and Sean look at a photo album and talk about family members.

- Tell your child where you are going. Children need to know if they are going to the park or to the dentist. Use a calendar with lots of visuals to explain and reinforce activities that will be happening in the future.

- Share information about how the family operates. Deaf children need to be taught about everyday activities such as checking accounts, writing checks, and paying bills.

- Talk to your child about events that are happening in the news. Be prepared to answer questions about what is happening. Your child may have missed some of the information. Share opinions with your child. Ask your child's opinion.

- Share feelings with your child. Tell your child why you are feeling happy or sad. Children will intuitively be aware of the emotional atmosphere in the home. They may blame themselves or come to erroneous conclusions if they do not understand the issue at hand.

- Share your values with your child. What is right and wrong? What is appropriate in a situation? What are good manners?

- Think about family gatherings. These can be difficult for a deaf child because there is so much activity. Think about how you can adjust the seating or the schedule to make it easier for your child. At large family gatherings, have groups of people arrive at intervals. This gives your deaf child a chance to connect with each person and adjust to the new situation.

Physical Environment

- Lighting is important to consider. You must have lights bright enough to make lipreading and reading signs easier. Deaf families generally have their houses more brightly lit than hearing families.

- Make sure that you have night lights in the children's bedrooms and in the bathroom and hallway. Deaf children become unnerved when it is dark and they can no longer rely on their vision.

- Young deaf children need to have visual access to Mom or Dad at all times. Keep the blinds open when you go out to get the mail. Deaf children can become frightened if their parents seem to suddenly disappear. Tell your child where you are going when you exit a room even if it's for a very short time. Hearing children monitor this information subconsciously with their hearing.

- Arrange the furniture so that conversations can take place with people facing each other. Face-to-face communication is optimal.

- Be aware of glare from the windows. It is difficult for a deaf person when the glare from a window is behind the speaker.

- Have a Telecommunication Device for the Deaf (TDD) and a captioned television available even for small children.

- Control the noise in the home. Background noise makes it difficult for the deaf child to use his or her residual hearing. The noise from a TV or radio will drown out any information the child might hear.

- Control the "visual noise." An environment that is too visually busy will distract the child from concentrating on lipreading and reading signs.

26

^^^

FAMILY PORTRAIT OF COMMUNICATION

The family portrait of communication that you design now will reach far into your family's future. As you begin to make decisions regarding communication, the blueprint you design will set the stage for communication in your home. Every family has a unique system for interacting with one another. Patterns and systems of communication are constructed in every family, whether planned or not. The way you communicate within the family unit will influence your deaf child and his or her family relationships for a lifetime.

The fact that you now have a deaf or hard-of-hearing child in your family means that you must now draw a communication blueprint that fully includes your deaf child. You may no longer take communication for granted. Instead, you must stop and think about how you are going to change your family interactions so that your deaf child is a part of every conversation. Consciously develop a system that includes your deaf child. If you do not consciously and consistently include your deaf child in your family communication system, he or she will not be written into the blueprint. This means that your deaf child will be the outsider in his or her own family.

We have often talked to deaf adults who are detached from their hearing families. This is the result of feelings of isolation that occurred repeatedly during their childhood. They were not an integral part of their family's communication system. They were always expected to make the effort to lip-read, to pay attention, and to extrapolate meaning and information from a situation. They were left outside the communication loop and often they missed the joke and were told, "Never mind. It's not important." The message is, "I don't have time to explain it to you," or "You are not important." When given that message repeatedly, it is a self-fulfilling prophecy.

Experiences of adults who become hard of hearing will help you understand what your child is facing. Adults in this predicament need to adjust to new communication difficulties. Their language system is already established. They are able to understand a conversation with one person at a time. However, these adults experience difficulty following conversations in a group. They begin to avoid meetings, parties, and other occasions where people gather because they cannot follow the conversation and feel left out. Suddenly, the communication system that they are familiar with does not function for them. Daily life becomes a struggle because of communication difficulties. They begin to make assumptions because they are left out of the communication loop. Sometimes hard-of-hearing adults become self-conscious and think people are talking about them because they perceive people as whispering. A person with a hearing loss can feel totally alone and isolated in a crowded room.

A deaf or hard-of-hearing child may feel alone and isolated in his or her own home because of these communication difficulties. Deaf adults often tell stories of situations in their own homes where they were lacking information. Many deaf children will isolate themselves purposely to avoid the situation. They may go off in a corner and watch TV at a family gathering because it is too difficult to participate.

Information that hearing children pick up automatically, such as family incidents, may be missed by a deaf child. One student came to school and told the teacher of a funeral he attended, but he didn't know the name of the person or the relationship. It was his own grandmother. You must think about how you are going to communicate in your home and adjust your communication so that your deaf child is a full participant in family matters.

In homes where deaf children are an integral part of the communication system, communicative stress is reduced. Fewer struggles, tantrums, frustrations, and physical tensions exist. Children who have received positive messages about communication in the family unit enjoy high levels of self-esteem. They have a lifelong bond with other family members. Furthermore, these deaf children have the confidence and self-assurance to participate readily outside their family in activities such as recreation and sports.

Remember that your family portrait cannot be designed by an outside contractor. Doctors, therapists, or school administrators cannot design a family portrait of communication. The communication interactions and language learning that take place in the home cannot be duplicated in school. In homes where the communication system is fully inclusive of the deaf child, close relationships and high expectations for the future are the norm. With a communication system in place, your family will travel together through daily life and some of the more challenging issues that deafness brings.

27

ONE FAMILY'S PORTRAIT

I knew that the task before us was enormous when at age twenty-four months my daughter, Meghan, was finally diagnosed. I was panicked. I didn't know how she would ever be able to catch up. Meghan lacked language at every level. She needed a tool belt of skills for communication and later literacy. Furthermore, without the ability to communicate, Meghan would never develop the ability to articulate her thoughts and needs.

An audiologist encouraged me to put Meghan in a program that used oral techniques exclusively. Given Meghan's strengths (visual and kinesthetic) and weaknesses (speech and listening), I knew this advice did not address her needs as a whole child. It was emphasizing her weaknesses not her strengths. Subtracting information in a modality that suited her to perfection would limit her ability to catch up in the communication skills that she so desperately needed. The sound of her voice was of little significance compared to the more important aspects of communicating her needs.

I made the decision to sign because it was apparent that Meghan needed a visual system to communicate with ease. I wanted to know about ideas that filled her head, her thoughts, and feelings. I wanted to connect with her. I couldn't wait any longer to experience the joys of communicating with my daughter.

Now I was faced with another issue—what sign system to use. I read many articles and learned the power of ASL. I was fascinated watching Deaf families sign and saw how my daughter was drawn to it. I knew that exposing her to ASL would also help her self-esteem because it would validate her deafness. It is important for her to recognize that she is deaf and that this rich culture has much to offer our family. Had I been a Deaf parent, the logical choice would have been for me to use ASL.

I began taking an ASL class and was overwhelmed with the enormity of learning an entirely new language quickly. Learning vocabulary was not difficult, but learning how to combine and connect phrases and sentences and gain grammatical competence was overwhelming. I soon began to realize that it would take me far too long to acquire proficiency in this new language. I knew that I had to be able to use this language fluently to give Meghan the communicative support that she needed. I knew that the best role model for her would be a native ASL signer. However, that would not solve our communication issues in our home.

I needed to find a sign system that would be easier to learn and would allow me to transmit the language of our home culture, English. I felt that a signed English system would meet these criteria. We began to learn Signing Exact English (SEE) as it met our criteria for communication in the home and was widely used in our area.

Using this sign system enabled us to establish reciprocity that was lacking when we used an oral-only approach. Using both speech and a signed English sign system simultaneously seemed a logical choice for my family. It would allow Meghan to develop her receptive language skills including the rules of English grammar and sentence formation. Simultaneously, Meghan would have the opportunity to develop her listening and speech skills to her full potential. Our tool belt for communication and literacy became complete with the use of both signed and spoken English.

As a bilingual educator, I knew that removing language from a child's repertoire has devastating effects on the child's cognitive, social, and emotional growth. This is called *subtractive bilingualism.* Contrary to what some people believe, language learning is enhanced when students are encouraged to use the language in which they are more comfortable. Therefore, I encouraged my daughter to sign, knowing that this would enhance her communication skills. Socially, signing would allow Meghan to converse and develop peer relationships. Meghan would also benefit emotionally by having a communication system to express her feelings. The positive reinforcement she gained through this communication mode was emotionally healthy. As she became more competent with signs, she gained the confidence to use her speech.

Both of my deaf children signed before they spoke. My son's signing began at eight months and his oral language began at eighteen months. Sean has had the luxury of acquiring both signed and spoken English naturally. By the time he was born, our household had already developed into a signing environment where he flourished. Our daughter, who did not have the luxury of both signed and spoken English in her home environment, showed the symptoms of language deprivation. I engaged in what I call "drill and kill" with her. Countless hours were spent with her strapped in a high chair drilling her on vocabulary. This technique worked somewhat because she was starved for language and was willing to endure it. In contrast, my son will tell a therapist in such a situation to go away or that he is finished. He has the language necessary to manipulate his environment and communicate his needs and desires.

Using SEE is only the beginning of our journey. Our competency and fluency in SEE has allowed us to connect with Deaf adults. Our children are naturally drawn to ASL and are integrating ASL principles into our home communication system. However, I look forward to the time when we are competent and fluent in ASL. It is fascinating to watch their natural development in sign. Our roles are changing and Meghan now leads the journey.

As a hearing parent of two deaf children, I can tell you that it is a demanding journey. As a bilingual educator, I already had an understanding of language acquisition and development, bilingual methodology, rich teaching experiences, and interactions with children of diverse backgrounds and special needs. Equipped with this knowledge and educational background, I still have my daily struggles. Communication constantly requires patience, time, and extra effort. It is true that I have moments when I feel as though I just can't make the extra effort to make these children understand. Yet I know that the effort, time, and patience that I practice now will give them the edge they need to be successful adults.

Often, parents are told that it is a hearing world and that deaf children need to learn how to live in it. As a hearing person, this is a powerful message because I want my children to be successful in my world. Even more important to me is that my children be in a place where they are comfortable, where communication is pleasurable, and where they know they are loved. My children will always know that I made the effort to provide a harmonious balance of speech and sign. They will have struggles communicating in a hearing world and I cannot shield them from these hardships. This is something that every deaf person must learn to deal with. This is part of the deafness and I cannot change it. However, I want their home to be a sanctuary, a safe place where they are valued for their unique attributes and not judged by the sound of their voice.

28

PASSING ON LANGUAGE

Life with infants and toddlers can be all consuming. Sometimes we become so immersed in the everyday tasks of caring for very young children that we forget the bigger picture. That bigger picture is what we foresee in the future. It is essential that your choices and decisions encompass a vision for your child. Think beyond your present circumstances and consider what tools are most important for your child to become a participating and contributing member of society. Decisions that you make now will affect your child for the rest of his or her life.

As your child's first and most important teacher, make sure that the home environment meets your deaf child's needs. The basic need of communication must be considered of primary importance. A deaf child's home should be an environment where he or she is able to learn language naturally and comprehensively.

Why is this important for you and your child? Deafness is more than a hearing problem. It is a communication problem. Many children with a hearing loss do not acquire high-level literacy/English skills when they get older. Parents become worried when their deaf or hard-of-hearing child cannot keep up academically with his or her hearing peers. However, the tools with which a child needs to be successful in school are acquired in the first five years of life. Most of this learning is done in the home by interacting with his or her parents, the child's first teachers.

Deaf children's language deficits have nothing to do with their cognitive potential. It is solely a communication problem, not a neurological problem. For this reason, it is disheartening that many deaf people make it to adulthood without having acquired a rich repertoire of English language. The problems they generally have with English do not revolve around vocabulary. It is more of a problem of putting the words together in correct English word order. They do not understand the underlying intricacies of the English language. They are unable to manipulate English in a native-like fashion. They have not internalized the basic design and patterns of the English language. For them, English is a difficult intellectual puzzle.

Evading the use of intricate language patterns with your deaf child deprives him or her of developing rich language. Many parents get bogged down in teaching vocabulary such as colors, shapes, foods, and animals. Vocabulary is a concrete structure of language and is easily learned by children. Although learning vocabulary is an important tool, it is an isolated piece of language learning. It is a surface feature of language and does not promote linguistic competence. Drilling children on language is not a pipeline to fluency.

It is far easier to use simple language with your deaf child. Whether you use ASL, signed English, or oral only, hearing parents often revert to simple language structures and vocabulary. It is important for you to go beyond the artificial properties often adopted by hearing parents so that you can truly be a language model for your child. You need to give your deaf child the same language experiences that you would give a hearing child. Engaging in natural conversation, modeling of appropriate language structures, using language creatively, reading to your child, and exposing your child to print of every variety are strategies that promote rich language development.

Children learn by being presented with language structures and information slightly beyond what they already know. You should be presenting language patterns slightly more complex than the patterns your child uses. This is a continual process and essential for your child's cognitive progression. Children who are challenged linguistically learn to think more creatively and flexibly. Children who think creatively and flexibly inevitably become competent readers and writers.

There is a critical period for learning language that lasts from birth to approximately six years of age. Children in this window of time acquire language rapidly, comprehensively, and aptly. We know that language learning in childhood is far easier than in later years. Children internalize the rules of grammar without any effort. They do not need to be taught or drilled. An example of this is when hearing children make mistakes in applying a rule of grammar. In English, we add -ed to most verbs to form the past tense. While children are internalizing the rules of grammar, they will add -ed to irregular verbs. Common examples of this are: haved, goed, and spended. Children who do not internalize the rules of language comprehensively and aptly during these years are forever at a disadvantage linguistically. The window of time in which language development occurs in children never recurs later in life. Even with intensive therapy, children who do not acquire intricate grammatical features in their early years seldom catch up.

There is a linguistic life cycle. Language maturation proceeds in a predictable sequence and must take place in a determined amount of time. If this does not happen, the critical period is missed and the opportunity to develop facility in language is missed. The brain changes to acquire different developmental skills.

Deaf and hard-of-hearing children are at particular risk in this linguistic life cycle. They are not getting the same quality and quantity of language as a hearing child who is absorbing it with no effort. Parents must make continual efforts to make language accessible in their home. During the first five years of life, systematic language must be installed in the deaf child. Hearing parents must install this language by adding the software themselves. This cannot be accomplished by sending your child to a special class a few mornings a week. If the vision you hold for your child is that of a participating and contributing member of society, then you must consider this responsibility of passing on language to your deaf child as the greatest gift that you can give your child. This pinnacle of time will soon disappear, so you must engage yourself fully. This is what makes the journey for hearing parents so challenging. It is a tremendous responsibility. Your child will not have the tools to achieve his or her fullest potential if language is not developed during this critical period of the linguistic life cycle.

This process of learning language is so natural with hearing children that we take it for granted. We don't even think about it or reflect on it unless some problem develops. Language development in hearing children is like acquiring teeth. Suddenly, baby teeth appear effortlessly at the appropriate time. In hearing children, there is a predictable order of language development. Most parents have no expertise in the area of language development, yet their children acquire the appropriate language structures at the appropriate time.

Hearing parents of deaf children must have knowledge of language development in order to give their deaf child a complete language system. They must be aware of the kind of input that they are modeling for the child. It cannot be a watered-down version of the same language they are giving their hearing child. Making substitutions because it simplifies your life and saves time is not a quality interaction. Dialoguing with your child in a complete fashion is essential. Using shortcuts to communicate with your deaf child is watered-down language. Your child will inherit these communication patterns.

I often have to remind myself to take the time to use challenging vocabulary and challenging language structures, even if I have to look up the word/endings. The sign language book lives on our kitchen counter just for this purpose. I am bothered by the fact that I am not a perfect language model but I teach my children that I, too, am a learner. It is important to take the time to promote quality language interactions in the home.

29

THE MIRACLE
OF LINGUISTIC
CREATIVITY

The miracle of linguistic creativity is like the beauty of a garden. This blossom of language begins with seeds planted and cultivated in the very first months of a child's life. The first blossoms of language in a child are a colorful and unique surprise. It is an intrinsic part of the bond between parent and child. Often we are not even aware of it on a conscious level. As the garden is sowed and cultivated, it flourishes in height, depth, and width, as does the language of a child. As a child asks and answers questions, shares opinions and observations about the world, and expresses feelings and emotions, his or her language flourishes.

Parents are the gardeners who tend to their children's linguistic needs by expanding upon that which is already growing. Just as you give flowers water, you give children the words and language they need. Some of the flowers in your garden require more tending than others. Sometimes the most beautiful ones require the most work. Signing requires more work on the part of a hearing parent. The benefits of providing rich and stimulating language experiences in sign reap a full harvest of language. It truly will not matter that the first blossoms of language in your child will not parallel the blossoms of hearing children. The blossoms that your child offers are unique and carry a beauty all their own. We all don't have to have red roses; some of us prefer purple iris.

You need to adapt the home environment to the needs of the child just as you adapt the soil to the needs of the plants in your garden. You do not grow cactus in the rain forest. Arrange your home and lifestyle to support and nurture your child's language. Your deaf child is an integral part of your family garden. He or she may require different types of language or care than another family member. You are the gardener. Provide for your deaf child in a way that encourages his or her unique attributes. No one else can accomplish this in your place. Nurture your child in a way that recognizes his or her linguistic needs. The sooner you establish an environment that facilitates language learning for your deaf child, the sooner you will have the privilege of watching your child flourish and grow.

The learning that takes place in the home now will be the foundation for a lifetime of concept development. Make this foundation of learning as rich and comprehensible as possible for your child. A hearing child gets meaning from incidental learning experiences such as overhearing conversations. A deaf child needs access to the same type of incidental learning situations. Though this may seem inconsequential, the efforts you make to construct a home environment that is fully comprehensible will give your deaf child control of language.

We make an effort to sign even our arguments so that our children do not miss the intricacies of language interaction. It is also important that they understand the context of the situation and the reason for the argument. Commonly, deaf children will misinterpret the reason for an argument and think they are the cause. Full communication teaches children many essential things about communication, from vocabulary and content to pausing and turn taking. This is quality communication.

By observing many language interactions, Meghan has learned to effectively communicate her frustration and anger over a broken teacup.

30

SPEECH/LISTENING STRATEGIES

There are many things that you as parents can do every day to make listening and speech an integral part of your deaf or hard-of-hearing child's life. These activities can be fun and playful. It should be something that you are doing automatically when you interact with your child in daily activities and routines. Speech and listening are interrelated. Your child develops speech skills as a result of listening and trying to imitate what he or she is hearing.

The objective in working with your child is to develop the physical abilities that enable him or her to form words and speak. These include:

- oral motor ability, which refers to the motor control to get the lips and tongue to make the necessary movements to make sounds

- listening skills to develop auditory memory for pitch changes, intonation patterns, vowels, and consonants, which are the basis for developing speech

The following activities can be incorporated into your daily routines to make listening and talking fun.

- Putting hearing aids on your child should become part of your dressing routine in the morning, just like putting on your shoes.

- Alert your child to listening by signing and saying, "Listen."

- Let your child control the presence or absence of sound. For example, let your child turn the blender or stereo on and off. Say and sign, "Listen, it's quiet or it's noisy."

- Call attention to environmental sounds in your home. Give your child the opportunity to hear these sounds many times so that he or she can begin to recognize the sounds and identify them. Can your child find where the sounds are coming from? For example, every time the phone rings or someone knocks on the door say and sign, "Listen, do your hear that? What is it?" Show the child where the sound is coming from and talk about the sound. Other examples could be a car horn, dogs barking, the blender, the vacuum cleaner, or objects dropping.

- Call your child's attention to voices in the environment. Call your child's name. Use the names of other members of the family. Can your child identify Mommy's voice or Daddy's voice? Can your child find where the voices are coming from?

- Use pictures of family members. Using listening, ask your child "Where's _____?" using the names to see if your child can recognize the names of family members.

- Use toys and objects that make sounds. Present the object and see if your child can find and identify the sounds.

- Talk to your child using intonation patterns that are pleasing to him or her. For example, if your child falls down, say, "Uh oh," or if your child is hurt, say "Ow." Encourage your child to imitate these easy-to-hear sound patterns. In the beginning, your child will imitate the intonation pattern of the speech rather than say specific words correctly. This follows normal development and should be encouraged.

- Find a particular sound that makes your child smile. When making that sound, tickle or touch your child in a way that engages him or her further. Sean loves the sound of trains and he made that sound before he said or signed the word. In frequently practicing the "choo, choo," Sean was able to articulate words such as "boo," "blue," "balloon," and "chew."

- Provide practice in speech by varying duration, intensity, and pitch of your voice.

    Duration—long vs. short sounds

    "baaaaaa" vs. "ba, ba, ba"

    - Pair a motion with the sound, that is, draw a long line or run your finger down your child's leg. Tap the pen or tap the baby's arm to the short sounds.

    - Pour milk or water—vocalize while you are pouring. Stop vocalizing when you stop pouring, that is "AHHHHHHHHHH" stop!

    - string beads—vocalize when pulling beads down the string.

    - vary the sounds you make. One day work on "ahh," then next day work on "oooo."

    Intensity — loud vs. soft sounds

    - whisper and talk in a loud voice

    - imitate quiet vocalizations and loud shrieks of your child

    - cats say "meow" (loud) vs. kittens say "meow meow" (soft)

    - dogs say "woof, woof" (loud) vs. puppies say "woof, woof" (soft)

– talk about loud sounds such as a car horn, or drum, or soft sounds such as a bird or water running

Pitch—varied intonation

– draw a line that goes up and down and change your voice to go with the line

– use "oo,oo,oo" for a fire engine siren, changing the pitch intonation patterns to go with emotional states

- Provide practice in listening and imitating speech by pairing specific speech sounds with an action (lifting your child in the air and saying "Up, up, up,") or a toy (the train goes "choo, choo"). You can work on vowels and consonants in this way. Keep the sounds that you use consistent with the object or action. Some other examples include:

  – animals and the sounds they make

  – other transportation sounds

  – sounds used in family routines, for example, "mmmm that's good," "up, up, up," "WOW," and "round and round"

- Sing familiar children's songs and do the appropriate hand motions. Encourage your child to follow along and sing along with the gestures and melody. Your child will learn to recognize the songs and you will know when he or she uses the hand gestures. Songs could include: "Twinkle, Twinkle Little Star," "Eensie Weensie Spider," and "Row, Row, Row Your Boat."

- Think about what events occur everyday. Plan sounds that cue the child to these activities and repeat in a consistent routine each day. For example "MMMM. It's time to eat." "Splash, splash. It's time for a bath."

- Developing breath control is very important for speech development. Have your child practice blowing through straws, blowing feathers or bubbles, and blowing out candles.

- Motor activities to help your child get control of his or her tongue and lips include:

    - eating foods with a variety of textures and consistencies

    - practicing placing the tongue on each side of the mouth and licking off food on the upper or lower lip

    - closing lips and sucking through a straw or sucking up spaghetti

    - imitating other tongue movements—sticking out the tongue and licking a popsicle

    - blowing bubbles, feathers, candles

    - drinking through a straw

- Combine different vowels and consonants together in vocal play.

    - ba, ba, ba or ma, ma, ma, boo, boo, boo, bee, bee, bee, pa, pa.

    - Vary long and short sounds.

    - Choose sounds that your child is already making and have your child imitate.

    - When your child is successful with sounds that he or she already produces, add sounds that are new.

    - Play with these sounds while dressing, playing with toys on the floor, or playing with your child on your lap and moving with the sounds.

- Collect a box of objects that use sounds/words that you are targeting this month. Play with the objects and sounds. Use the objects for listening, by placing them on the floor and saying the words/sounds and seeing if your child can find the correct object. Have the child say the words/sounds.

- Play wake-up games—pretend the child or a stuffed animal is sleeping. Use different sounds—a horn, bells, yelling, clapping—to wake up the child or stuffed animal. Have some loud sounds and some more quiet sounds.

- Let your child listen to music and dance to the music. Feel the music through the stereo speakers.

- Beat a drum to a special beat. Have your child imitate the number or pattern of the beats. Beat a pattern on your child's arm or back and have the child copy the pattern on your arm or back.

- Discriminate words—fill a box with objects or pictures of words you are working on. Practice saying the words.

- Practice listening and speech with two syllable words that have different vowel sounds, for example, ice-cream vs. toothbrush. Play with the words and sounds. See if your child can choose the appropriate object when you say the word using listening alone.

- Practice listening and speech with one-syllable words with different consonants and vowels, for example, dog vs. cat or doll vs. truck.

- Practice listening and speech with words that have the same vowel sounds and different consonants, for example, dog vs. frog or man vs. pan.

- Practice listening and speech with words that have different vowel sounds and the same consonants, for example, dog vs. dad or mom vs. mop.

- Practice giving your child familiar directions using predictable language that you use every day using listening alone. Choose five to ten directions that you use often, for example, "It's time for dinner." or "Go get in the car." or "It's bath time." or "Turn off the light."

- Make a listening activity when reading a book. Say the words and have your child point to the pictures and say the words.

31

SIGN STRATEGIES

In a deaf child of deaf parents, signs appear spontaneously and predictably. This is because sign has been modeled on a consistent basis. Similar to hearing babies, deaf babies will babble with their hands and engage in baby signing. Baby signs are early forms of adult signs. In speech, a baby may use an early form of the word bottle by saying, "Ba ba." A deaf child may use an early form of the sign mother by tapping the chin rather than having an extended hand. Baby signs are a part of sign development and should be positively reinforced and encouraged.

The first sign usually appears two to three months before a hearing child's first spoken word. A child's sign vocabulary and number of signs develop faster than oral language in a hearing child. It is typical for a ten-month-old deaf baby to have a sign vocabulary of 10–15 signs. A hearing child does not usually say his or her first word until a year. Signs develop from iconic to abstract. An iconic sign is a sign that looks like an object. Some examples include ball, airplane, telephone, and tree. Abstract signs, which have no visual reference, include more, want, and let.

As a deaf child becomes more competent with signs, more difficult finger positions are achieved. This is the development of true signs and it will take time. As your child sees you make the correct sign, he or she will become a more competent signer. Deaf children are able to put together two sign expressions at about a year and three word phrases at age eighteen months to two years. Signs are to a deaf child what words are to a hearing child. Signs allow for communication, comments, reflections, thoughts, and cognition. Although sign is a different mode than spoken language, it feeds the mind and soul of a deaf child as words do to a hearing child.

Following are suggestions for optimizing sign language learning.

- Keep a sign book handy at all times, on the kitchen counter, in the glove box of your car, and on the family room table.

- Encourage your child to handle the sign book and look at the pictures and words. Encourage older children to look up signs you don't know.

- Put the manual alphabet in a location accessible to your child, for example, on a wall low enough for your child to look at and touch the hand shapes. Even very young children will sit and try to make the hand shapes.

- Use lots of pointing to clarify what you are saying. "Pick up the doll" (point to the doll).

- Use a facial expression. This is an important part of signing and conveys meaning.

- Use body language to act out what you are saying. If you are saying the word "tired," express tired with your whole body.

- Sign what your child is doing. Sign what you are doing.

- Sign background conversation.

- Sign at your child's level and make it easy and interesting for your child to watch you.

135

- Respond to your child when he or she initiates a conversation.

- Draw your child's attention in a positive manner. Try not to grab, startle, or move your child's chin to get his or her attention.

- Look up signs before embarking on any adventure. Take advantage of learning opportunities.

- Read and sign books to your child. You may need to look up signs before you read a book. Reading a book many times will satisfy a child's need for repetition and your need for reinforcement.

- Begin signing food words at mealtime. It is rewarding for children to be able to request food items that they want or to reject items they don't want.

- Be sure to use the connector words such as for, to, in, out, and at.

- Use prefixes and suffixes.

- Provide your child with books about deafness and signing.

- Purchase or make up sign language games.

- Attend church or community events with interpreters.

- Watch movies and TV shows with closed captions. Interpret your child's favorite TV show.

- Use signs that include time and sequence—tomorrow, before, after, later, next, and in the morning.

- Make analogies and comparisons: "The pillow is as soft as your bear." "Your pants are smaller than Meghan's."

- Use signs that imply quantity: "That is too much cereal in my bowl." "There are too many cookies on my plate." "That is not enough milk in my cup."

- Use sign structures that include cause and effect: "If you leave the cookies in the oven, they will burn." "If you leave your bike outside in the rain, it will get wet."

- Use sign structures that include position and direction. Position your hands so that the meaning is clear. "Your socks are under the chair." "Your ball is behind the couch."

- Use words that can be used in many different ways in English. These words are signed differently in ASL. When using a signed English system, ASL principles should be adopted to differentiate the meaning; for example, "Run an errand." "Run around the track." "Run for office." "Run in your stocking."

- If you are using simultaneous communication methods, speak and sign at the same time. The signs will support the use of speech. The signs help your child understand speech. For example "goat" and "boat" sound alike. By signing, the child can readily understand the difference.

- Incorporate finger spelling in your signing. Finger spelling facilitates literacy. Deaf parents finger spell with their children at an early age. Begin spelling little words that your child is familiar with, such as cat, dog, or people's names. The child will recognize the hand shape and movement before seeing individual letters.

- Begin connecting letters on the hands with letters in printed form: street signs, books, or language cards.

32

~~~~~~

LANGUAGE FLUENCY

A child's language fluency evolves from daily interactions with his or her parents and other key people. The communication you share with your child should be concrete and simple at first. Your child must be able to fully comprehend the message. A child shows that he or she understands a message through facial expressions or nodding or by appropriately following the directions or responding verbally. Communicating at this level is where your child functions independently. Initially, your child's independent language level may be limited to simple words such as "eat," "go," or "up." It is important that you identify your child's independent functioning level so that you can provide communication that is at an optimal pace and level.

Working with your child within this comprehension zone leads to language progression. When a child has fully understood a concept and that concept has become a part of his or her knowledge base, the child is ready for something slightly more complex. This is where learning actually takes place. Expand on your child's signs or utterances by adding a new word or making an analogy. Don't expect an immediate response. Your child will need lots of reinforcement before the next concept or word becomes part of his or her knowledge base.

Be sure to remain alert for your child's attempts at language. Ensure that your body language encourages your child to initiate conversation. Smile, pause, and give good eye contact and your child will learn that you are expecting communication. Imitating your child encourages him or her to take the lead in conversations. It also gives your child the message that you are proud and interested in what he or she has to say. Even imitating sounds that your child makes, such as car sounds or animal sounds, gives a positive message about language. Every attempt at communication, nonverbal or verbal, that is positively reinforced will feed your child's appetite to communicate.

When your child initiates a conversation, besides positively reinforcing the attempt, keep the conversation going. Continue positive body language, eye contact, and physical contact. Do everything you can to make your child feel competent. Even if you don't know what he or she is trying to communicate, make sure you remain engaged. Take a few guesses from the environmental cues (is your child wet, hurt, hungry, thirsty, dirty, or in need of a special blanket or toy?).

The essence of communication is that you have an interest in what your child has to say. Be careful not to control the conversation. Be a partner rather than a lecturer. Allow your child to guide the conversation. Other times, take the lead but be sure to remain natural. Stilted speech and exaggeration may confuse your child. Remember that your child will inherit your communication patterns.

Structure and routine in the home can help support your child's communication. Using consistent language predictably will give your child some of the tools necessary to develop his or her vocabulary. Structure and routine in the home does not need to be rigid. Make routines fit your lifestyle. Predictable routines allow for consistent environmental cues leading to understanding.

A strategy to incorporate into your household routines is the use of pivot words "more" and "want" when a child is requesting. Use these pivot words often and predictably. Use these words in situations that are meaningful for the child, such as at the table to request food or at play to request toys or activities. Begin with easy concrete words in the routine of your household. As your child internalizes these words and begins to express them, use words that challenge your child to control his or her environment. These words give your child power. For example, the word "mine" is very powerful. It can be used in a variety of situations and will enable your child to think beyond a simple label.

Many parents spend a lot of time teaching "label words," for example, ball, cracker, dog. These words are concrete and easier to teach and learn. Challenge your child with words that provide higher thinking skills. Other examples include: help me, move, watch, look, or finished. These words can be applied in a variety of situations and can be used to manipulate people in the environment. If a child does not want to do an activity anymore, being able to say, "Finished" is more appropriate and powerful than throwing the toys on the floor. "Finish" can also be used when a child does not want to eat anymore or wants to get out of the bathtub. The child can use this word with linguistic flexibility. These words help children understand that language is a tool to get what they want. When you establish a language routine in your home, deaf children accelerate their language learning.

Hearing children have many more opportunities to acquire language naturally through their environment. Working with a deaf or hard-of-hearing child takes more time and energy. Hearing children can learn so many things incidentally. A deaf or hard-of-hearing child misses many of these opportunities due to hearing loss. A parent of a deaf child has to manipulate the situation or learning task so that the child has the opportunity to acquire language. Parents and teachers can set up the environment for maximum learning.

For example, bath time is part of a normal routine with your child. Use this opportunity to promote language. As you set your child in the water, sign, hot, cold, warm, water, bubbles—a lot, or a few. Sign "blow" and do it. Splash, talk about wet and dry. Have a big boat and a little boat, reinforce big and little with the signs, and put people in and out of the boat, under the water, or floating on top. Allow the child to initiate the play and give the child the signs for what he or she is doing. Allow for response time and positively reinforce any response that the child gives. If the child signs boat, kiss him or her, clap, and praise his or her efforts. This repetition is important at the time and also subsequently to reinforce the concepts. Do it several nights in a row and then change the toy; for example, get a duck—a big duck and a little duck. Then go through the same activities adding something different to see if your child can generalize the language.

Good communication in the home makes children more confident and able to manipulate language effectively. For example, my six year old faces the challenges of a fully included academic situation. In order for her to be successful in this environment, she needs to be able to take risks. She is not afraid to join in a discussion and participate in class because she has had many successful experiences with communication. Deaf children need an extra dose of encouragement and acceptance because just the looks on people's faces tell them that they are different. Children with high self-esteem who have been nurtured and encouraged and accepted for who they are are much more able to face life's challenges.

33

HARMONIOUS BALANCE OF SPEECH AND SIGN

A mutual language between parent and child must exist for their relationship to develop throughout a lifetime. In a family where everyone is English speaking and is hearing, everyone is speaking English to communicate. There is no need to adapt or change the language to make sure that everyone is in the communication loop. By the same token, if everyone in the family is deaf, then the use of a manual language for communication is obvious. Speech is usually not used and if it is, signs often accompany it. Everyone in the family understands and uses signs with ease, and communicative challenges are lessened.

The situation is more complicated when some family members are deaf or hard of hearing and some family members are hearing. If the parents are deaf and the children are hearing, signs may be used in the home. However, the deaf parents may use speech or compensate in other ways when their children bring friends home or when they are interfacing with their children's school. Deaf parents often support the development of good oral English skills for their hearing children as well as encourage facile communication in sign.

In families where the parents and other family members are hearing and only one member is deaf, hearing family members must adapt the communicative environment to include the deaf person. Because 75 percent of the words spoken cannot be read on the lips with any degree of accuracy, the use of signs will logically play a significant role in family interactions. Signs are the stepping-stone to the very special place where deaf and hearing people may communicate with comfort and ease. Signing can link family members in a mutually beneficial way. It lays the pathway for bonding in a family with both deaf and hearing members.

Speech is the most natural vehicle for communication for hearing people, and they feel most comfortable using it. Hearing people rarely substitute the ease of using spoken English to use signs without voice. Most deaf people will not give up the ease of communication using signs to use speech exclusively. Therefore, it seems that in a family with both hearing and deaf members, both signs and speech will be used in the home. Communication in the home must embrace all family members.

If everyone in the family considers quality communication important, a harmonious balance of speech and sign will develop. This balance will be different for every family. Families that use both speech and sign readily are in a paradigm where all members and languages are valued. Deaf children learn early that the spoken word is more widely used and appears to hold more status than their signs. Embrace a communication system that values both signs and speech.

Families who have made the paradigm shift see that the language mode of each family member is valued. Celebrate the unique gifts each member brings. Travel the bridge that will connect and bond your family. Arrive to the paradigm where language bonds, not separates, family members.

As you construct an inclusive family communication system, you will experience many revelations. One of the first is the shift in how you view your child. In a paradigm where all members, both hearing and deaf, are appreciated, a deaf child is no longer handicapped or disabled. He or she is a participating, contributing, and integral member of the family. In this paradigm, the deaf family member is a whole person, not a broken-hearing child.

Another revelation you will experience is regarding the opportunity your deaf child awards you. You can gain access through learning and practicing signs to another culture, the Deaf culture. Embrace the new opportunities and experiences offered you. Be thankful for these unique insights and learning. Realize that the new dynamics in your family are healthy, both emotionally and socially. Allow each member to thrive in an environment that is supportive and respectful of language and culture. Enjoy the creativity and multiple abilities of every family member.

There are many voices in the field of deaf education. Some will be positive about your family practices and others will be negative. Not all deaf adults agree that speech should be used with sign. People who encourage an auditory/oral perspective will say if you sign, it will be impossible to give your child the practice in listening and speech that your child needs to develop fluent oral English skills. Signing can slow down speech, but practice in simultaneous delivery will make it smoother. Signers who are trying to sign a correct model of English often are able to sign every word in correct grammatical order. Simultaneously speaking and signing English is just another way to support English. Adults often slow down their speech on purpose because they want their children to see all the grammatical elements of communication. They learn to do this in natural and efficient ways.

It takes a lot of concentration and practice to speak and sign correct English word order, vocabulary, and grammar at the same time. You can do it if English proficiency is your goal. You must realize that you will not be a perfect model all the time; no one is. Sometimes the use of speech will be more important than the signs. Some situations will require your child to use listening and speech reading. Sometimes the signs will take precedence and you will not use your voice. This may be especially important when you are teaching a new concept or are in a confusing, noisy environment.

As a family with both hearing and deaf family members, you need to develop a harmonious balance of speech and sign that will uniquely fit your family. Using both signed and spoken English is one way to include all family members in the communication loop. Speech and signs will both be used in your home because you have family members who use each for communication. Therefore, you must decide how your family will integrate both spoken and signed communication. Developing a harmonious balance of speech and sign is a challenge for all families with both hearing and deaf members. Developing a system that includes all family members will enhance your family communication.

34

~~~~~~

PRIOR KNOWLEDGE

Prior knowledge is important in establishing higher learning skills. Students with lots of general knowledge about the world, different experiences in exploring their environment, and rich vocabularies have, in essence, large bank accounts. When teachers begin lessons, they frequently use questioning or brainstorming strategies to tap their students' prior knowledge. Teachers who know where their students' functioning level is can proceed at a comfortable learning rate. Students who present high levels of prior knowledge have accelerated learning rates. Teachers may proceed far more rapidly through learning when students bring lots of basic background knowledge to the learning environment.

This knowledge base can be acquired quite easily in the home in a nurturing environment. Most parents are experts in building prior knowledge. When a parent of a hearing child takes him or her to the grocery store, many incidental conversations occur that build prior knowledge. For example, a trip through the produce section of the store may result in incidental learning, such as apples grow on trees, farmers pick apples and ship them to the grocery store, and there are many different kinds of apples with many different names. The child may also learn that apples are fruit and are used to make applesauce, candy apples, and apple pies.

This prior knowledge can then be applied to understanding other fruits and vegetables, how they get to the store, and what they are used for. A deaf child may leave the store with a new label for an object, "apple." All the other information may be missed due to the fact that it takes more time and energy for the parent to explain things to a deaf child. Consequently, a valuable opportunity to build prior knowledge is missed. A parent of a deaf child must be prepared to take advantage of these kinds of opportunities. Parents must be proactive and strategic in bringing basic concepts to their children. A deaf child does not just "pick up language." Parents must plan and predict what language they can bring their child in a natural and nurturing way. Look up a few key signs before embarking on any adventure and then

A child's knowledge base is constructed through cooperative play and then reinforced by independent exploration.

capitalize on learning situations that may present themselves. A pocket-size sign book for the car may be helpful.

The best way to build prior knowledge in a child is to follow his or her own lead. My son is fascinated with trains. After he learned the sign for train, I began introducing different kinds of trains beginning with simple attributes such as long and short. Frequently, in stopping to watch a train on our way home, we began discussing whether the train was long or short. At home, we built long and short trains. After Sean understood long and short, we moved on to other attributes—things the train carries, where its parts are located, the names of the cars, and speed. Sean has currently exhausted the cumulative knowledge base on trains of his parents, sister, and teachers and is thankfully moving on to airplanes. His knowledge of trains is accelerating his learning of airplanes. Because he knows that trains have conductors, he readily understands the function of a pilot. Sean was thrilled to find out that airplanes have wheels, "Same as trains," he signed.

35

TEACHING VOCABULARY

Building a good vocabulary base will help your deaf or hard-of-hearing child when he or she begins reading. Words that your child knows and uses in conversation can be transferred easily to knowing and understanding the same words in print. Don't limit your child by using a limited vocabulary. A deaf child may understand chair and sit, but the words stool, couch, armchair, sofa, or the names of different kinds of chairs may be unfamiliar.

Teaching your child vocabulary is a good place to begin developing English language skills. Most vocabulary that you start with will be concrete and easy to teach. It is helpful to teach words in categories because the child will learn to group together words with similar properties. These categories include: animals, clothing, foods, toys, furniture, tools, colors, shapes, vehicles, and common verbs. Look up the signs for the group of words that you will be focusing on for the week or month. Think of activities that will highlight these words. Experience is the best teacher. Going on a train ride or visiting a farm will have more meaning for your child and the words will be remembered better because of the experience. Take pictures of the trip so that you can talk about what happened and review the vocabulary that you are teaching. Look for books or pictures that will illustrate the words you are teaching. You can act out many common verbs. Adding adverbs, adjectives, prepositions, and conjunctions will increase your child's ability to use the English language and make simple sentences.

Abstract words or concepts also need to be taught. You can teach children about feelings—sorrow, happiness, anger, and frustration—by describing your feelings or your child's feelings in a particular situation. Concepts such as empty/full, many/few, big/small, and tall/short, can also be taught by using the words in appropriate situations.

For example, teach "empty" one day by showing your child empty containers. You have lots of empty dishes in your kitchen. When your child understands that concept, teach "full" by filling containers. You may need to repeat the activity several times before your child understands and uses the word. Hearing children hear a word many times in context before they use it. Deaf and hard-of-hearing children need more repetition in meaningful situations to develop an understanding of these concepts.

Idioms can cause confusion for deaf or hard-of-hearing children because of their abstract properties. Idioms must be taught and explained to deaf children. Consider teenage slang and the difficulty many adults have in understanding the idioms they invent. Idioms are part of our culture and are used frequently and with great flexibility. Idiomatic phrases such as "pipe down," "cool it," and "get over it" are abstract uses of language and need to be explicitly taught. Deaf children enjoy learning about idioms and how to use them. Giving your children information about the use of idioms helps them to feel competent and capable. Once children understand the abstract quality of idioms, they will be able to apply this knowledge to the written word. Your child will encounter these phrases in many types of literature.

Similar to idiomatic phrases are words with multiple meanings. Words such as "fire" can be used in many ways. For example you could say, "The fire is hot," or "I was fired from my job," or "The man fired a gun." These types of words can be very confusing and even funny for a deaf child when they only know the word in one context. Often, the words are signed not as a word but as a concept. Therefore, even though "fire" is used in all three sentences, it is often signed three different ways to make the concept and meaning of the sentence understood. Some deaf children don't realize that this word can be used in a variety of instances with different meanings until they see it in print. By that time, many deaf children are at a disadvantage because they are not linguistically flexible and have become rigid in how they comprehend words. Exposing your child to the multiple meanings of English words will help your child master social language and comprehend the written word with more clarity.

It is possible to know all the words in the English dictionary and still not be able to speak English. You must know how to assemble words into sentences. Knowing the grammar of English is what allows us to make sentences that can be understood by others.

As very young children, we begin to figure out the grammatical rules that govern English. We learn how to ask questions, how to say no, how to request, how to make past tenses and plurals, and how to make some ideas depend on others. Knowing these rules allows a child to generate sentences that will communicate wants, such as asking for a toy, protesting when he or she can't have what is wanted, or planning an activity. Constructing a knowledge base with lots of experiences with words of every variety will facilitate communication and comprehension for a lifetime.

36

~~~~~~

GRAMMATICAL COMPETENCE

G rammatical competence is an essential feature of fluency in English. Deaf children sometimes lag behind their hearing peers in their acquisition of grammatical constructs of English. Children become grammatically competent by meaningful exposure to language. Hearing children learn through a process of listening to conversation in their environment. As they make errors and learn to correct these errors, they achieve closer approximations to correct grammatical structures. In order for deaf children to become proficient readers and writers, they must first internalize the grammar of the English language.

All children go through stages in learning the rules of grammar. Children progress through these stages as they practice communicating, and adults provide models of correct grammatical forms in their answers. Deaf children sometimes miss some of the intricate grammatical features of language due to their hearing loss and lack of meaningful exposure. Deaf or hard-of-hearing children cannot always hear grammatical features of English, such as endings of words, and many adults don't sign them consistently. Adults can assist children who are deaf or hard of hearing by modeling grammatically correct English when talking, signing, and reading with them. If a child questions or comments with an incorrect grammatical phrase, an adult can use the correct form in the response. Adults can also ask children to repeat what was modeled to help internalize the correct form of English.

The syntax describes the parts of the sentence and the order in which they are arranged. Word order plays an important role in being able to understand English. The way the words are arranged can change the meaning completely. Consider this example:

The boy pushed the girl.

The girl pushed the boy.

Push the boy and girl in the swing.

The meaning in the sentence is completely changed by the word order. A string of words arranged in a certain order makes a sentence. Various rules are followed, such as agreement between subject and verb, the addition of tenses, and plurals. Deaf children need to have correct and complete English sentences modeled for them. They need to learn how the word order of English affects the meaning of the sentence.

Word endings or derivations also change the meaning of a sentence. For example, the word "electric" changes to the word "electricity" when it is used as a noun. Verb inflections are the changes in words such as come, came, comes, and coming that are a part of correct English grammar. Deaf children do not always hear these subtle differences in words and many adults do not sign these differences. Therefore, many deaf children do not use them when they speak or recognize the differences in print.

153

Certain grammatical structures can also be difficult for deaf children. They often leave out transition words such as at, to, and for. This easily changes the meaning of an English sentence. Pronouns, articles, and auxiliaries are sometimes misused or left out of sentences. These little words are hard to lip-read and are often left out when signing is used. If you model these words to your deaf child, he or she will begin to incorporate these words into communication. If a child can use these words appropriately in communication, he or she will be able to transfer this information easily to the reading process.

The use of the verb "to be" can also cause confusion. Traditionally, there have been no signs for this verb. However, in English, this verb is used often. Children need to see how it is used naturally in English. By modeling the use of is, am, are, was, were, and been, children will learn which pronouns go with these words. They will also learn when and how to use these words. The agreement of the verb and pronoun can be taught. However, this results in more stilted language than when children internalize the rules for usage themselves.

Deaf children generally understand simple declarative sentences. However, when simple sentences are changed to a more complex form, they may become more difficult for a deaf child to understand. For example, passive voice, negation, questions, compound sentences, or prepositional phrases may confuse a deaf child.

The boy is building a tower with blocks (simple sentence).

A tower of blocks is being built by the boy (passive voice).

The boy is not building a tower of blocks (negation).

154

Is the boy building a tower of blocks (question)?

The boy is using blocks to build a tower (prepositional phrase).

The boy is building a tower and he is using blocks (compound sentence).

Another essential component of English is the extrapolation of meaning from a sentence or phrase. This is called *semantics*. For example, it is easy to describe the various tenses used in English. However, it is often difficult to figure out the meaning conveyed by these tenses. Time is the semantic component and understanding the meaning of the time in the sentence can be complex. For example, the sentence "Bob leaves tomorrow," uses present tense but refers to the future. Present tense can also be used to describe actions that took place in the past such as, "Bob looks at Linda, then turns away and boards the plane." Understanding tenses and the semantic component, the time the action takes place, can be a challenge to deaf children.

A more mature deaf or hard-of-hearing child who is struggling with English grammar may benefit from the use of visual tools, such as graphic organizers, to internalize English grammar rules. Pictures can illustrate the specific derivations of a word such as "come." Fold a paper into four or eight boxes and have your child draw a picture of the word below it. On the next box, use another derivation of the word and a slightly different picture that illustrates the word change. The pictures should be very simple but clearly emphasize the word change in each box. Another idea is to make word books. Design a book that uses one word and its derivations repeatedly. This book can be silly and fun for the child to make. Use the word "bring" and discuss all of its derivations in a fun story format.

Graphic organizers can also be used to illustrate complex sentences. Design a graphic organizer suited to your child's interest or personality. Create a suitcase with pockets for verbs, subjects, and objects. It can also be as simple as drawing two boxes connected with the word "and." The child draws pictures in the boxes to illustrate a compound sentence. The boy ate dinner "and" went to bed.

Modeling correct grammar through a signed English system and exposing your child to a variety of English words, grammatical structures, and complex sentences will help your child develop a grasp of English syntax. Explaining the meaning of sentences will help your child understand the semantics of the English language.

37

SOCIAL LANGUAGE

Most hearing children pick up on the social graces of language quite easily. Staying on topic, turn taking, and pausing in conversation are examples of the social aspects involved in communicating. We teach children social skills for communicating when we ask them to not interrupt or to use please and thank you. Another example of the social function of language is when we ask a child who is deaf or hard of hearing to speak more clearly or to make a request a second time, having been unsuccessful the first.

Deaf or hard-of-hearing children occasionally experience challenges in communication when their conversational style is abrupt. A deaf child may engage a person without using some of the necessary pleasantries or elaborations that hearing people normally expect. For example, a deaf child might request a pencil by tapping a classmate and saying, "Give me a pencil." The deaf child's body language might be insistent. The child may be uncomfortably close and use eye contact that insists on immediate attention. Unknowingly, the deaf child may have interrupted the teacher or the student's conversation. A hearing student may interpret this as rude and decide that the deaf child is not a child he or she would choose to play with.

In the English language, requests are made at appropriate intervals. Hearing children may have learned from example to wait for a pause in conversation, and insert a request for a pencil. This request will begin with social graces such as "Excuse me," "May I please?" or "Do you mind if I borrow your pencil?" Following the conversation, the recipient of the pencil will continue with social language by thanking the giver. This is a skill that hearing children may have acquired without formal instruction. Mastering the appropriate use of social language is a result of practice. Children who are deaf or hard of hearing often need to be taught these pleasantries directly or see them modeled in sign in many instances over many opportunities.

Deaf children must also have the language strategies that enable them to cajole, persuade, convince, or influence another person. The ability to use language in this way is an important social skill that can be elusive to deaf children. A child who has internalized the strategic components of language can do things such as paraphrase, restate, argue, or debate an idea.

Deaf or hard-of-hearing children need to have strategic language strategies installed in their language repertoire. Deaf children sometimes have trouble engaging an adult appropriately and relating their needs, opinions, and point of view. A young deaf child quickly resorts to physical contact to engage another person. This abrupt style may work with other deaf children but is not socially accepted in a hearing environment. A deaf child needs lots of reinforcement in methods of initiating conversations. Hearing parents of a deaf child are sometimes taken aback when their child abruptly engages another child or adult. Overcoming this abruptness for a deaf child can be a challenge. Try to exercise patience. It is not a reflection of your competence as a parent nor is it your child's fault. This is part of the learning process. Gently correct your child, encouraging him or her to use appropriate language and actions.

Children learn to manipulate language to get their needs met. A young child will use smiles, cuddles, and sweet language to engage an adult. At other times, young children will have a tantrum when they don't have the words they need. A four or five year old will use repetitive language phrases and will entice an adult with such persistence. A child of age nine or ten will justify or make analogies: "Tommy's mom lets him ..."A teenager uses strategic verbal skills to present an inductive argument.

A deaf child may also need language to interact socially with peers. Deaf children can be left behind in peer interactions if they are unable to coax or entice friends to their point of view. Older deaf children may also struggle with how to strategically insert themselves into a peer conversation or a classroom discussion appropriately. We can help them by role-playing situations in which they ask for a review of the topic or practice interjecting an appropriate comment.

Deaf children may have difficulty engaging themselves in a discussion that demands that they articulate their opinions so as to influence others. They need to know when to use their language to ask for a paraphrase or a clarification of what the teacher just said. A deaf child needs to know and have the confidence to say, "I didn't understand what you said. Could you repeat that?"

Parents might not be aware of the importance of strategic language competence in children. Hearing children acquire this information subconsciously because they have access to all the communication around them and they have more opportunities to practice. For example, when a mother takes her children to McDonald's, the hearing child is encouraged to order for himself. After the child practices the language and he is successful, he gets his Happy Meal, a perfect reward. If the child is having difficulties, adults jump in and coach the child in appropriate strategies. Contrastingly, a hearing parent of a deaf child often orders for the child without even asking the child what he or she wants and without giving the child an opportunity to practice strategic language. These skills carry over into adulthood, allowing us to ask for a raise in a strategic manner, bargain for a new car, and confront problems at the office or in social situations.

In a local restaurant, kids eat free on Wednesday nights. The menu is limited, allowing the children familiarity with the choices. On these nights, the children practice skills in engaging the waitress and requesting their menu choice. Another family made a "generic menu" with foods the children liked and would often order. This menu served as a tool for ordering in any restaurant. It allowed the children security in knowing they could get their request fulfilled.

Social skills are important for interpersonal communication. In a deaf or hard-of-hearing child, this means being able to navigate the playground, get to the rest room, or ask for a cookie. Performing socially is a skill that requires practice and reinforcement. Though these skills are more easily learned by a hearing child, they require a lot of practice with verbal interactions for a deaf child.

38

ACADEMIC LANGUAGE

By the time a child begins speaking a language, momentous amounts of learning have taken place. For hearing children, this natural learning process has been spontaneous and subconscious. Deaf children do not always have the luxury of acquiring this foundational learning naturally due to the weak auditory channel.

Deaf or hard-of-hearing children often lack language for the academic environment. By the nature of a child's hearing loss, they have not had the same opportunities to engage in verbal interactions that would allow them to be more cognitively flexible with the English language. Learning in the classroom depends on a child's ability to use language creatively. Children must be able to generate unique thoughts and explain them. Deaf children who have not progressed from the concrete properties of language into abstract thinking skills are not able to generate and explain new ideas. Deaf children who have not been exposed to substantial amounts of comprehensible and complete language are at a disadvantage academically.

Many people believe that the deaf child who has good speech will have an academic advantage. Good speech skills are not always correlated to high academic achievement. Children with good speech skills are sometimes at a disadvantage. The language that they need the most has been overlooked because they appear so fluent orally. These children may be deprived of the language skills they need to be fluent in cognitively demanding situations. It is often a surprise to parents when their children who are especially skilled in oral articulation have difficulty in a mainstream or full inclusion environment.

Cognitive language ability refers to skills essential for problem solving: comparing and contrasting ideas, applying knowledge to different situations, making inferences, understanding cause and effect, and clarifying ideas. Specifically, cognitive language happens when a child is able to recall past learning and apply that to a new, slightly different circumstance. In the classroom, cognitive language is evident when a child is able to recall a story, compare characters from the story to a new story, and make correlations between plots, themes, or morals.

Children need to practice manipulating language and sharing their ideas, talking about objects, and getting feedback regarding their predictions and thoughts. Ask your children what they need to take to school, and give them feedback on their response. I recall one day when Sean wanted to bring a potato to school. This baffled me and instead of simply telling him "no," I asked him why he thought he should pack a potato in his backpack. In his cryptic early language, he explained that he did not like the snack at school and wanted potatoes instead. This practice in language lays the groundwork for further experimentation with language essential for higher thinking skills.

Young deaf children benefit from learning situations that expose them to concepts such as comparing and contrasting, patterning, categorizing, and predicting. The first step in establishing cognitive language in children is giving them concrete labels in their environment. Once children can name objects, they need to be able to describe the attributes of the object. Next, the child needs to experience other objects with distinct similarities and differences. Encouraging children to talk about "how things are alike" and "how things are different" gives them practice in higher level thinking skills such as categorizing and comparing and contrasting.

The visual properties of sign allow many deaf children an alternative path to drawing conclusions. Deaf children may be able to see a correlation by making a visual picture with their hands or mind or on paper. A hearing child may make the same correlation by speaking or writing. Navigating demanding language tasks in a classroom can be a challenge for a deaf child who has not had enough practice in accessing language for cognitive purposes.

It is essential to prompt your child to use language to build on his or her thoughts. Effective language learning happens when your child has a grasp of the concept (such as comparing how things are alike) and understands the English you are using (how are these objects alike?). Children need lots of practice in meaningful situations to advance cognitively in their language ability. Deaf children who have been continuously encouraged to make verbal connections in their thinking are at ease in cognitively demanding situations such as the classroom. Following are some ideas to encourage your child to stretch beyond the present level of cognitive functioning. Use the prompts in situations that are real. Make them a learning experience that is natural and relevant to your child's life. Hands-on learning that is meaningful provides your child with the mechanism to succeed in an academically challenging environment.

Prompts for higher level thinking skills:

- **What will happen if ...**
  I leave the cookies in the oven too long?

I drop the glass? the Christmas ornament?
I don't turn off the water in the bathtub?
I don't feed the dog? I don't water the grass?
I leave this bread on the counter for two weeks?

- **What do I need ...**
  to open the can?
  to start the car? open the door?
  to make a cake? a milkshake?
  to go to the beach? to the park? to school?

- **What do you think is inside ...**
  Mommy's purse? Daddy's pocket?
  the beach bag? the lunch box?
  a barn? a pet store? a toy box?
  a closet? a drawer? a refrigerator?
  the witch's kettle? Santa's bag?

- **Why do you think ...**
  the boy is crying? the girl is happy? Mom is mad?
  the dog is barking? the bird is digging in the grass?
  you should wear boots today? a coat? a swimsuit?
  Daddy is late? Sister is in bed today?
  the bus is not coming today? we are staying home today?

Meghan has social language abilities in both oral English and signed English. She is able to participate with her hearing peers in following classroom routines and procedures and on the playground. Unlike her hearing peers, she does not have the cognitive language in oral English to complete cognitively demanding tasks. Frequently, she signs as she reads to paint the kinesthetic and visual pictures in her mind for reading comprehension. Signs allow her to compete on a cognitive language level parallel to but unique from that of her hearing peers.

39

~~~~~~

DISCOURSE COMPETENCE

C hildren learn many subtleties and intricacies of communication besides learning the labels for objects and how to get basic needs met. When children are engaged in conversations, they learn subconsciously how to be competent in the discourse of language. Mastering the art of discourse competence is a challenge for many deaf children. Many times, deaf children have not had as much experience engaged in conversations as hearing children.

In order for children to be communicatively competent, they must have internalized the pattern of the language. This means being able to engage in dialogues using the correct sequence and order of thoughts. Every language has a unique pattern for expressing thoughts and ideas. This is called the *discourse pattern of the language.* Children who have mastered the discourse pattern of a language can comprehensibly and cohesively put thoughts together. Children naturally and subconsciously acquire information about the pattern of the language they have practiced.

The pattern of English is linear and deductive. As we speak, we form our thoughts in concrete terms beginning with the most important thought first. When we speak and write, we give the main idea first and then add the details or the supporting arguments.

Different languages have different discourse patterns. Children learn how to manipulate language patterns early. Very young children will begin with the most important piece of information first. For example, a child will say, "He hit me." When questioned, a child will defend himself by giving details of what happened. Frequently, you hear things such as "I hit him because he pushed me." These children unconsciously are engaging in deductive reasoning. It is what they have listened to and experienced in their culture. In order to get their needs met, they have learned in how to engage in the linear and deductive language patterns of English.

Deaf children must practice how to engage in conversation in a deductive and linear fashion to develop their English language skills. Conversing in this manner may not come naturally to your deaf child. However, it is an important skill that will have far-reaching impact on his or her ability to problem-solve, to read, and to write. Comprehension of the written word demands that the reader has internalized the basic design and pattern of English. Children's stories at the most basic level require an understanding of how thoughts and ideas are organized.

When discussing issues with your deaf child, make sure that you begin with the most important idea first and then follow it with supporting information. For example, "You must be careful around the bee, because it can sting you and that will hurt. Bees are good because they make honey. They are also good for flowers."

Supporting ideas or concepts with details is important in developing the appropriate patterns used in English. Practice thinking aloud. Talk to yourself aloud about some of your deductive thoughts. This will positively impact your child's cognitive development. For example, if you are planning a trip to the grocery store, think/sign aloud making sure that your deaf child is internalizing the information. "It's time to go to the store. I must find my grocery list. After I find my grocery list, we will check it again. Next, we will need our jackets from the closet. We will put our jackets on and get the car keys." Using similar strategies will assist your child in developing the thinking and communicative processes necessary to engage in the appropriate discourse pattern of English.

As you can see, by the time children achieve fluency in a language, they have mastered momentous amounts of essential information for communicating. These elements include grammatical competence, strategic competence, social competence, academic language competence, and discourse competence. Installing all this knowledge in a deaf child is a daunting task, yet these aspects of language competence must be considered by a hearing parent of a deaf child. Deaf children who have a parent who has seen to their language needs are at a definite advantage socially, emotionally, and academically.

40

READING TOGETHER

My son enjoys sitting on his Richard Scarry book, *The Biggest Word Book Ever.* This book is made of baby board pages taller than he is. He loves the transportation page filled with airplanes, trains, boats, trailers, and tractors. He signs, voices, laughs, and points to the familiar objects and then asks me to sign, voice, and point out others. I encourage him to turn the page but we must always return to the same page and repeat the same ritual. This book is no longer in book format. The pages have come apart at the binding because Sean has either lain or sat upon it too many times. Yet he continues to enjoy the pages, perhaps even more now. He is attached to this book and his ownership is so deep that I am the only one besides himself who can touch it. No matter how dreadful this book becomes, I don't think we will ever be able to part with it. His attachment has become contagious. Meghan is his private security guard for the book and doesn't allow any of the neighborhood kids near it even if it is underfoot. This poor book has suffered every punishment imaginable, yet it becomes more endearing to all of us.

Children cannot learn to hold a book and turn the pages properly until they are developmentally ready to do so and have had the experience of developing an attachment to and ownership of a book. Your modeling of appropriate book handling will be their best guide.

Sean's enjoyment of this big book sets the stage for later literacy success.

Twelve to Twenty-Four Months

Between twelve and twenty-four months of age, children often begin to develop a curiosity for a particular theme. Examples are bugs, birds, stars, or the moon. Capitalize on your child's interests. Wordless picture books on a single theme conveying a simple story are good choices for this age. Picture books, such as the *Carl* books, convey a whole story without using the printed word. The object of these books is to work on a child's vocabulary and language skills while introducing sequencing. The pictures must be looked at in sequence, and sequencing is an essential part of reading comprehension. Picture books are especially useful for hearing parents of deaf or hard-of-hearing children. They allow you to sign in a fluid manner, using signs that are familiar to you. It is important to enjoy books in a comfortable and creative way.

Establish a flexible routine for reading. Children at this age are incredibly active and easily distracted. Choose a time when the child is looking for security and closeness and is tired enough to stay reasonably calm. The physical closeness or snuggling is as important as the story. Make story time a positive ritual. Adjust it to your child's attention span and give stories in doses that are ample but not overkill. Don't feel as though you must always finish a book. When your child begins to show signs of boredom or becomes interested in something else, simply stop. Adjust books and story time to your child's moods. Try to set a positive tone. Find at least one consistent time, such as bedtime, to read each day.

Focusing and listening are acquired skills that develop gradually. Give your child some time to settle down and get ready to focus and listen. Positively reinforce your child when he or she is focused. This doesn't need to be a big deal; a heartfelt hug works beautifully. Show your interest in the book and model the behaviors you want to see. For example, talk about where to begin, and turn the pages appropriately. When your child has the book right side up, tell him or her that is the right way to begin. Next, turn the page appropriately. When your child does this, reinforce this behavior. At this age, it is essential that your child has many opportunities to handle books. Make sure that your easy-reach library is accessible to your child. Leave interesting books in areas that your child frequents during the day—small tables, chairs, even the floor. If your child displays an interest in a book, go with it!

Positioning a deaf or hard-of-hearing child to see the book as well as your signs may take a little experimentation on your part. It may seen awkward at first. Be creative!

We enjoy sitting in my daughter's daybed with lots of pillows. Each child sits on either side of me and slightly forward. This allows the children to watch my face and hands and also gives them access to the book, which I hold in my lap or leaning against a pillow in front of me. The children can then point and comment on the book, each at his or her respective level. Meghan will point out words and help me read repetitive phrases while Sean points to the illustrations and will imitate signs. Each child takes a turn turning the pages. Having one child on either side of me helps reduce squabbles and gives me access to both of them and the book. Likewise, they can both see the book, it's print and illustrations, and my signs. My husband likes to lie in bed with the kids with a book propped on a pillow board in front of them. Be warned that this method is most conducive to sleep, for adults especially. I always know when I hear little pajamaed feet walking down the hall that Papa has fallen asleep in their bed!

Small kid-size tables are also helpful in getting down to your child's level. Put the book on the table and sit either next to or directly across from your child. It is important to make sure that the book is right side up for the child and that he or she has access to the illustrations and print.

41

SUPPORTING LITERACY

Begin a home library for your deaf child as soon as possible. Visit secondhand stores, thrift shops, and garage sales. Check your local public school and library for discarded books. These books, though outdated, can be an essential part of your "hands-on" library—a collection of books that are accessible to a child at all times. These books must be available to a child to experience the book on his or her terms, even if it means tearing a page or eating it. If a child is never allowed to handle a book until done to adult satisfaction, precious time will have been wasted in the reading process. Concepts about print are learned at this stage as a child handles a book and discovers which end is up and how to turn the pages. This kind of discovery should be encouraged and never reprimanded. You will go through many books, but in the process, valuable learning will take place naturally.

The hands-on collection of books should be inexpensive or hand-me-down books. They may also be durable, toddler-friendly books. These books are the ones that can be loved in real kid fashion. Allow your child to have books that he or she may sleep with, lie outside under a tree with, or even drool upon. Babies and toddlers must have plenty of opportunities to feel books, look at books, sleep with books, and even eat books. This is how babies and toddlers develop ownership for a book, which gives them a sense of security. There is nothing wrong with a child having a security blanket made of paper. This ownership or attachment to books is a cornerstone in building literacy. Making books an integral part of your son's or daughter's life is a gift that is multi-dimensional and will serve your child for his or her lifetime.

Besides a hands-on library, you will want to begin to develop a "high-shelf" book library. These books are to be shared only with an adult. They should be handled with care at all times and then put in a safe place with the child's assistance at the end of each reading. High-shelf books should be visually within reach of the child but not in hand's grasp. Although they should be respected, these books should not be out of sight. Visual access is important so that children don't forget about them and have an opportunity to ask for a favorite book.

Before my children were born, I began collecting some of my favorite children's books for them. These books all contain special messages to my children and hold an extra-special place in our respected home book library. Give your child a special book for each birthday and encourage family members and close friends to do the same. Write a special message to your child in these books. In birthday book messages, I like to include what qualities I like best about my children, recent milestones and accomplishments, a description of what they look like, their likes and dislikes, and who their special friends are. I also tape a photograph of my child on that birthday in the book. I sometimes will choose a book because a character reminds me of my child or shares the same interest or challenge. Deaf children should be exposed to books that have positive deaf role models. Books are a relatively inexpensive gift and are important pieces to literacy. When parents share a special book with a child, they share a piece of themselves, which is the best gift of all.

Birthday heirloom books, autographed books, and expensive books should be placed on shelves that are visible but out of the reach of dirty fingers, drippy noses, and color crayons. Make sure that the "special books," though out of reach, are within sight. They will serve as a kind of goal. By treating these books with extra respect, you will be modeling the importance of good literature and the important role it plays in our growth as individuals. Pull these books out when you have a quiet, tranquil moment to spend with your child. Occasionally, after my normally well-behaved daughter has been reprimanded, I will sit quietly with her and pull out one of my favorite books. This ritual always puts us in better spirits and again teaches her the power of a good story.

Between six and ten months of age, a child begins to recognize familiar faces and objects. Therefore, your book selections should be picture books with large, colorful pictures of familiar faces and objects such as people, dogs, trains or cars. Books such as *Where's Spot?* encourage parents and babies to interact with the story. In this charming series of stories, children manipulate sturdy, movable flaps to uncover surprises. Picture books that allow children to touch or smell or lift things are sure to engage even a toddler with a limited attention span. Plot is not of importance at this stage. Engaging your child with books that reflect their environment are the most useful. Deaf children at this age are able to recognize simple signs.

Sign on top of objects in books that your child is familiar with. Simple, bold, colorful objects in solid colors of red, yellow, blue, and green against a plain background are best. Other selections should include babies doing familiar activities: drinking from a bottle or cup, eating a cracker, feeding a duck, or going to sleep. Durable baby board books that fit in the grasp of tiny hands and can be wiped clean after being drooled upon are also good first-year choices. Many books have holes that children can manipulate or interesting fabrics to touch. Be creative and make books with and for your child. Put photographs in small, clear sandwich bags and glue them onto cardboard. Choose themes for your books such as eating, dressing, or taking a bath, or about family members. Talk about each picture with your child. Do this repeatedly, allowing your child to hold and touch the pages.

Incorporate finger spelling into your reading routine. Point out letters and sign on top of them. Look for books that have signs depicted. After you sign a word such as "up," finger spell it. Before long, your child will begin to make the connection between the printed letter and the letter formed on your hand. Later, this knowledge will transfer to the recognition of longer words and sentences. Deaf children often finger spell a word long before hearing children are even exposed to the idea of spelling.

42

~~~~~~

READING ROUTINES

Around age two, children begin to acquire more book etiquette. They can occasionally be left to do some "independent" book exploration, especially if they have had a lot of previous experience with books. It is important to lead by example because children are fabulous parrots at this age. Begin to point out some of the words you read and sign. It is okay to sign with one hand. I find it easiest to point to a word with my left hand and sign it with my right hand. Pointing to the words you read teaches your child many important concepts about print. Pointing as you read teaches a child about the left to right directionality of the English language. Most importantly, pointing to words as you read them teaches a child that print is talk written down. People are always fascinated with children who appear to have taught themselves to read. Although these children have not had formal instruction in reading, they have had wonderful role models who have unknowingly taught them. Kindergartners who come to school already reading, or students who respond readily to instruction in reading, have inevitably had access to a wide variety of printed material and have been read to on a regular basis.

It is amazing to me that Meghan reads as well as she does, considering the substantial delay she experienced in acquiring language. Books and print have always held a prominent place in our home and she was always read to on a regular basis. Furthermore, her grandmother enjoys spoiling her by walking her to the bookstore and allowing her to pick out any book she wants.

If your child's language is also delayed, don't be discouraged. Children have amazing cognitive flexibility and can catch up. Begin reading to your child on a regular basis and his or her first steps to literacy will be taken.

A child of two or three years can begin to enjoy other types of printed materials. *Baby Bug* and *Ladybug* are excellent magazines filled with stories and activities for a very young child. My son has a basket of birthday cards, kept with his easy-reach books, that he loves to play with. These cards have pictures that are fun and familiar to a toddler. They also have names at the bottom and we talk about the people who gave him the card. A child's name is usually the first printed word he or she can recognize, so introducing the names of important people in the child's life is a good strategy toward developing literacy.

Your child will also begin experimenting with crayons, paper, and pencil at this age. Begin writing your child's name in big, bold letters on all of his or her work. Sign each letter as you say it. Tell your child, "This is your name," and run his or her finger under it. Post your child's work in a place where it can be seen frequently. The refrigerator or a bulletin board at your child's level is perfect. In schools, we make an effort to create print-rich environments where students can literally read the walls. Use this same strategy at home by displaying your child's work and labeling it.

Introduce your child to nursery rhymes. Act them out. As you recite, sign, or read *Humpty Dumpty*, use a real egg to demonstrate. Your child will love it. Repeat it often so that it begins to hold meaning for your child. Children's bookstores and teacher supply stores carry stuffed objects to accompany many fairy tales. As you read a story such as *Goldilocks*, give your child a Papa Bear, a Mama Bear, and a Baby Bear. Use all of the visual aids you can think of. Nursery rhymes and fairy tales are an important part of our culture. Many teachers will assume that their students have been exposed to some of these even before entering school. Make an effort to integrate fairy tales and nursery rhymes into your child's repertoire.

At this age, your child is also acquiring a sense of humor and knows when things are silly. My son thinks his book about the potty is hilarious. I, of course, was hoping it would provide him with a knowledge base to help him achieve this all-important milestone. Although he has not yet transferred this knowledge to a real-life situation, he has learned another concept about books—they are fun. Other book choices for this age are books about daily routines. *All By Myself*, *Froggie Gets Dressed*, and *My Book About Me* are books with which a two to three year old can identify.

Concepts about print are entirely accessible to a three year old. Children at this age who have been exposed to print are capable of listening and watching a story. At age three, a gap already appears between children who have been exposed to books and those who have not. Your child should begin to show an appetite for books by this age. It is more important to give your child a desire and love for books than to try to teach him or her to actually read. If your deaf or hard-of-hearing child begins school with an appetite for books and an anticipation and excitement for reading, then the actual process of attaining literacy will be enhanced.

43

EXTENDING LITERACY

Once a child begins school, he or she must have the ability to follow the sequence of events in a story, visualize the characters, and recognize the major theme or idea. A child in the early elementary years should anticipate a story, expecting to find out who is in it, what will happen, and why. The child should also be able to give a personal judgment on the book, how much he or she liked it, and whether it was suited to his or her interests.

One of the most important skills for reading is forming mental pictures from the written word. This is not an easy task for deaf readers nor does it emerge automatically. In the home, this reading skill can be cultivated and nurtured in a fun and creative way. Creating vivid impressions of the literature you are sharing with your child is one of the most significant skills you can develop in your child.

First, help your child to organize the sequence of events in a story. Discuss or draw the beginning, middle, and end of the story. Use bright colors and elicit your child's ideas. Cut out the pictures, mix them up, and have the child put them in order and tell the story using the pictures. Be as creative as possible using fabric, real coins, buttons, or other materials to illustrate important points. Remember, you are trying to make a vivid impression! Another way to do this with a small child is with sidewalk chalk on pavement outdoors. Children who are kinesthetically motivated will enjoy the outdoor mural effect of a story.

As your child grows, your story mapping should become more complex. Use a computer and graphics to illustrate the sequence of events in a story, major themes, and characters. Have your child create a doll to match his or her favorite character. Encourage your child to use the character doll to retell the story. Allow your child to see a clip of a video of a book you are reading to facilitate the mental process of visualizing the written word. Once your child is motivated and involved with the story, stop the video and pick up the book. Soon your child will learn that the images one creates from the written word are more to his or her liking than the depiction on the video. Share with your child times you were disappointed with a movie because the characters you created in your mind as you read were far more interesting than the characters someone else created.

Bring your child to theater dramatizations of stories and compare and contrast these to the book. Make a diagram depicting the similarities and differences. Stories such as *Cinderella* are wonderful for this purpose. There are many different versions of the story and your child will gain a deeper understanding of the plot and theme from exposure to various versions. *The Three Little Pigs* is another story with many versions and now there is even a story from the wolf's point of view. My second-grade class adored the wolf's version and created a dramatization of the story with the wolf being "framed." Such experiences bring joy to the written word and give a child an appetite to experience more literature.

Books with repetition are also accessible and fun. These books give deaf children important reinforcement while allowing them to experience success. With these books, you may want to read the more difficult parts while your child reads the repetitious passage. My favorite pattern books are *Love You Forever; Now One Foot, Now the Other; The Very Hungry Caterpillar;* and *The Napping House.*

Children of all ages should be read to. Reading to children teaches them essential components of reading, even after they are able to read themselves. Pauses, intonation, and inflection are learned by being read to. Reading to children also gives them the message that they are important and you have time for them. As you read to your school-aged child, point out pieces of the written word that may be puzzling. For example, explain that the word "knife" has a silent "k," as does the word "knock." Make these mini lessons informative but very short; you don't want to disrupt the story. Other incidental learning you may want to point out to your child may be the use of dialogues when someone is talking or the use of punctuation such as an exclamation point. Make these impromptu lessons interesting and then immediately move on.

Another way to give the written word status is to model reading. By simply reading in your child's presence on a daily basis, you illustrate the importance of reading. Your child may naturally want to read simply because you show interest in it yourself. As you read the newspaper, point out pictures and articles that may be of particular interest to your child. Our daughter has a particular appetite for natural disasters. She loves learning about tornadoes, earthquakes, droughts, and fires. When we find an article with one of these themes, we allow her to cut it out and spend time talking about what happened. We give her a yellow highlighter and as we read, she underlines "disaster words" because they are interesting to her. Next, we get a map or globe and show her where the disaster occurred. We read the newspaper in the morning and frequently she reminds us in the evening that we must watch the news to see if there are any further developments.

The closed captioning usually shows some of the same "disaster words" we highlighted in the morning newspaper, reinforcing important vocabulary.

Writing can be used as another tool to enhance reading skills. Creating books for gifts is a wonderful way to celebrate the written word. In school, we use a technique called *interactive writing*. This is simply done by sharing the pencil with the child. Allow children to write the words they know and then guide them through words that they are unfamiliar with. For longer words, you may want to write them yourself. This form of writing gives children ownership of the written word because it is their talk written down. Recently, we created a counting book for a young niece as a gift. The children went through old photographs that for one reason or another were not photo album quality. They cut out pictures of people's feet and made a counting page for feet. Next, they decided on a page of hats for counting hats. Other pages included photos of cars, and themselves. In the process of creating the book, they learned how to read and write numerous words and learned important concepts about books such as how to create a dedication and make a title page.

Another strategy is to incorporate the written word into your daily lives in meaningful ways. My children enjoy leaving notes for my husband. These notes are simple but carry important messages. My husband was tickled to find a note on the kitchen table one morning that said, "Papa, please go get McDonald's for breakfast, we must eat." I occasionally include little notes and secret messages in lunch boxes or backpacks. Writing simple letters to grandparents or other family members also gives significance to the written word. Letters can be as short as one sentence such as "My grandmother is special because ..." The natural reaction that a person has over a letter a child has created is the best possible form of reinforcement.

Understanding the written word is especially important for deaf children as it is their pipeline to information they may not pick up. Closed captioning is wonderful reinforcement of the concept of reading being talk written down. In the early elementary years, assisting a child to read the closed captioning while watching TV or a video can be frustrating. Hearing children can simply sit in front of the TV and listen and watch quite passively and completely understand what is going on. A deaf child or hard-of-hearing child needs to be signed to and simultaneously have important words on the closed captioning pointed out. I sign what is happening in the show and then point out words that are developmentally within their grasp. As the children become more proficient in reading the closed captioning, I sign less and less. Occasionally, we will watch a wordless cartoon such as *Tom and Jerry* and I will have the kids sign what is happening. Allowing the children to mentally process and sign the words in a wordless cartoon is another technique for increasing comprehension.

The teletypewriter (TTY) is another essential tool in a deaf-friendly home that provides a powerful connection to the reading process. Children who are exposed early to a TTY learn that reading and writing provide links to other people in meaningful ways. Children who use TTYs regularly receive meaningful practice in conversing and relaying their thoughts in a cohesive fashion. Take the time to connect your child to others through the use of the TTY and they will be intrinsically motivated to read and write for communication purposes.

44

~~~~~~

LINKING LANGUAGE AND LITERACY

There is a logical progression from learning a language receptively to reading a language. A hearing child progresses from listening to speaking and from speaking to reading and writing. A hearing child must listen to a language for an extended period of time before he or she is able to speak it. A child must have several years of speaking experience before he or she is able to read a language. Writing a language follows the reading process. To interrupt this natural progression is to interfere with a child's intellectual development and disrupt academic potential.

The natural progression from receptive language to literacy for a deaf child is somewhat different, yet the process and chronology are similar. Deaf children must see signs for an extended period before they are able to sign and they must have a strong sign foundation for the reading and writing processes. Using both sign and speech for communication is a tool for the reading and writing processes. Hearing children take a giant step into the world of literacy when they come to understand that the written word is simply the words we say in print. When a child makes the connection between the spoken word and the printed word, he or she has acquired essential knowledge for reading. Deaf or hard-of-hearing children must come to understand that the words they make on their hands and the words they speak are the same words on the printed page. Depending on the amount of residual hearing, deaf students will have varying success with the connection between oral language and written language. If the child is exposed in sign to the same language that he or she encounters in print, the reading process is enhanced. This language and discourse matching will facilitate the reading process and allow for the natural order of concept development to occur.

If a child who is exposed only to the spoken Spanish language attempts to read the English language, a poor connection between the language used for communication and the language used for literacy development will be made. The result of this mismatch will be weak reading skills. Students who are literate in Spanish, with strong verbal skills and the ability to think abstractly, can transfer this ability and knowledge readily to English. These students are successful in their primary language and only need to re-label and move their vocabulary and thinking ability on to another language. Their first teachers, their parents, have passed on complete, consistent, and comprehensible language. These competencies transfer from language to language.

Deaf students who use ASL do not have the luxury of following the complete chronology of a bilingual model because there is no written form of ASL. Thus, deaf students must progress from communicating in ASL to reading English.

A child exposed only to ASL who attempts to read English may encounter difficulties in the reading process due to the differences in the languages, such as grammar and discourse pattern. The discourse pattern of English and the discourse pattern of ASL are not the same. For example, ASL uses a different word order than English and does not use articles such as *the*, *a*, or *an*. When a child begins to read, he or she may encounter difficulties because ASL is not a mirror of written English. In other words, the signs on a deaf child's hands do not match the printed word. The word order of English and the way that thoughts are organized on paper deductively may confuse the child. When a child comes across words in print that he or she has never experienced, the child may encounter difficulties in the reading process because these words have not been used in communication. The child may encounter difficulties in comprehension.

However, a deaf child with a rich language background and cognitive ability can overcome these difficulties. Similar to the Spanish-speaking student discussed previously, this child has a repertoire of strong verbal skills and the ability to think abstractly. These children often come from Deaf families who use ASL in a complete and consistent manner. ASL is their primary language and these children have developed competencies necessary to cross the bridge to English literacy. Frequently, deaf children of Deaf parents have been read to and have received positive messages about themselves and the learning process. In addition, they have had continual exposure to very positive role models, their parents.

The recipe for success is not quite the same for a deaf child from a hearing family. Children from hearing families need to have good language role models in the home. Hearing parents who are not fluent in ASL cannot provide the same kind of language and role modeling to their deaf child. As your child's first teacher, the most consistent and complete language you can transmit to your child will be English. Therefore, it may be more logical for hearing parents to begin with a sign system that fits their situation and models English. The transition from oral and signed communication to written word is cohesive and meaningful.

If you choose not to sign with your child, he or she must also follow the logical order to literacy. The child must listen for an extended period of time before speaking. This is done by using amplification and training the child to use residual hearing. The ability to use their residual hearing varies for deaf children. Some children will be able to learn this way. However, many will be delayed in the entire process. No one can tell you which child will be successful and which child will have difficulty learning through listening alone. It is important to consider the long-term effects of delaying this process on the child's cognitive ability and literacy.

In order to progress and achieve in education, deaf children must have a strong language foundation. Children who have not been exposed to signs may lack some essential tools for their literacy tool belt. The kinesthetic modality is helpful to all children learning to read and essential for deaf children to develop a complete language system. Deaf children who are placed in a Total Communication program but only see signs at school may also have difficulty. A child cannot get enough language input unless he or she is getting the language modeled consistently at home.

The complex English language must be used consistently and completely for deaf or hard-of-hearing children to be able to access abstract concepts. Deaf and hard-of-hearing children must practice to have competence in grammar, discourse, and social and academic language. The reading process presents far more obstacles to deaf or hard-of-hearing children who are not competent users of the English language. The child's tool belt for literacy lacks the essential tools to build strong reading skills if deaf or hard-of-hearing children do not have this foundation in language. As the parent, you must take responsibility for developing strong language skills in your deaf or hard-of-hearing child.

QUESTIONS AND ANSWERS

How many children are classified as deaf?

Deafness is not common in children. One out of every one thousand babies is born with a profound hearing loss. Approximately one-half of the causes are genetic; most causes of genetic deafness are recessive genes and many parents are unaware of deafness in other relatives. Over 90 percent of deaf children are born to hearing parents.

Does a child's hearing loss change?

Generally a hearing loss does not improve. Sometimes it appears that a child's loss has improved because the child has learned to use residual hearing and participate in a hearing test. As children get older, they sometimes lose hearing. This can be devastating for parents. Consistent audiological care is important in detecting any changes in your child's hearing loss.

Will my child talk?

The ability to speak varies greatly in deaf children. Some of the factors that affect the ability to speak include the amount of residual hearing, motor control and consistent amplification, the child's innate ability, the amount of practice, and the child's personality. A deaf child's speech should never be used as a ruler to measure his or her intellect or potential.

How useful is my child's audiogram in determining his or her educational placement?

An audiogram is only one piece of information. Many other factors play significant roles in determining your child's educational needs. Children who are visual learners will want to use a sign system to access information. Other children may be gifted at using their residual hearing and may be auditory learners even though they have a hearing loss. Children should not be placed in programs on the basis of an audiogram alone.

How do I know which educational approach is best for my child?

There is no method that is optimal for all children. Exposing your child to all options and observing his or her responses in both speech and sign is a realistic way to find the approach that meets your child's needs. Allow your child to be the guide. Formulate a program that is tailored to your child's unique needs.

Why is there controversy in the field of education for deaf children?

The controversy is based on a fundamental disagreement about deafness. The Deaf community views itself as a cultural and linguistic minority. The auditory/oral community views deafness as a medical problem that needs to be fixed. Therefore, education is somewhat polarized due to these perspectives. The Deaf community promotes the use of ASL and embraces positive self-concept. The oral community promotes integration into hearing society through the use of residual hearing and speech. As a hearing parent faced with this dilemma, know that you do not have to choose one or the other. Take advantage of what each has to offer your deaf child.

Do hard-of-hearing children have special needs?

Yes. Many hard-of-hearing children slip between the cracks due to their good speech and ability to appear as if they understand. Many of these children are mainstreamed and the teachers do not understand the complexities of even a moderate loss. Their needs appear minimal and they often do not receive the needed support to achieve to their highest potential.

Is it common for a deaf child to have other special needs?

Deaf children may have other special needs just as any other child. These include learning disabilities, motor problems, or emotional problems. If you have concerns about your child's development, speak to your child's teacher and request assessment in the areas of concern.

Can deaf students attend college?

Definitely. Deaf students have a myriad of options for higher education. Many colleges and universities have programs specially designed for deaf students. Deaf students may attend a college of their choice and receive the services of an interpreter and/or a note taker. Gallaudet University is the only university in the world designed to meet the needs of the Deaf.

Will I ever be able to accept my child's deafness?

Deafness is an integral part of your child. It is imperative that you accept the deafness and come to see the beauty of it. Your child's self-esteem is a reflection of the image you hold of him or her. Continue to read, share, and talk about the deafness. Adjust to this new perspective along your own time line and in a way that is meaningful to you. Your lifelong dreams and the joys your child will bring you have a new unexpected quality. Enjoy!

GLOSSARY

Adventitious hearing loss a hearing loss that occurs after birth, usually as a result of illness or injury.

Articulation the act or manner in which sounds are pronounced.

Atresia closure of the ear canal or absence of an ear opening.

Audiogram records on a graph the child's responses to a variety of sounds from low to high pitch and at various levels of loudness.

Audiologic evaluation tests tests conducted to determine whether a hearing loss is present, the severity and type of hearing loss, and which tones (pitches) are affected. They involve recommendations for the best way of dealing with the hearing loss, which would include selection of appropriate hearing aids.

Auditory training a broad term used when speaking of developing the maximum use of a person's residual hearing.

Aural a method of teaching that stresses proper amplification and development of listening skills.

Bimodal communication uses both signed and spoken English.

Binaural amplification two completely separate hearing aids; one for each ear.

Cochlea shaped like a snail, the organ of hearing located in the inner ear.

Conductive hearing loss hearing loss caused by pathology of the outer or middle ear.

Congenital deafness deafness present at birth.

Deaf when used with a capital "D," refers to a person who is culturally deaf; that is, one who participates in and contributes to the Deaf community.

Degree of hearing loss a scale that may be divided into seven degrees in which normal degree of loss measures 0–15 dB, slight = 15–25 dB, mild = 25–40 dB, moderate = 40–55 dB, moderately-severe = 55–70 dB, severe = 70–90 dB, profound = 90 + dB.

Distortion a faulty reproduction of sound, which may be caused by internal components, or by a failing battery.

Ear mold an individually fitted plastic mold with a channel to carry sound from the receiver into the ear. Usually fitted by the hearing aid dispenser and made by a laboratory or manufacturing firm. Worn in the opening of the outer ear.

Expressive language any form of communication used to convey ideas, feelings, or thoughts. This includes the language of signs as well as speech and writing. Expressive language comes after the child has receptive language.

Feedback the shrill whistling sound made when the hearing aid microphone and receiver are too close together, or when the ear mold does not fit properly or is damaged.

Frequency (Pitch) the measurement in hertz (Hz) of vibrations or cycles per second of sound. Most speech sounds fall within the "speech range" of 250 to 4,000 Hz.

Gain the decibel amount of amplification (difference between input signal and output signal) in a hearing aid.

Intensity the level of sound that we perceive or hear as loudness.

Intonation the rise and fall in pitch of the voice in speech.

Localization turning in the direction of or locating the sound source.

Maximum Power Output (MPO) the greatest intensity of sound a particular hearing aid is set to produce.

Mixed hearing loss a hearing loss that is partly sensorineural and partly conductive. A child with a sensorineural loss, for example, could also have a conductive loss from fluid in the ear caused by a middle ear infection. The result would be a mixed hearing loss.

Monaural one hearing aid, fitted only to one ear.

Nerve deafness (sensorineural hearing loss) deafness caused by a problem in the inner ear or acoustic nerve.

Postlingual deafness deafness occurring after the child has learned to talk.

Prelingual deafness deafness that occurs before the basic speech and language patterns are developed—usually before two or three years of age.

Receptive language the language that is understood by a person. This must be present before we can expect expressive language to develop.

Residual hearing the amount of hearing available in a person with a hearing loss.

Speech the use of breath, vocal cords, tongue, lips, and teeth to form words.

Threshold the softest sound a person can hear.

Total Communication an approach to language development that consists of the simultaneous use of amplification, speech, signs, finger spelling, gestures, and writing.

Tympanometry (impedance audiometry) this test measures the ability of the middle ear to conduct sound to the inner ear. Otologists use this test to help determine if a middle ear problem exists.

RECOMMENDED READING

Adam, A.J., Fortier, P., Schiel, G., Smith, M., Soland, C., and Stone, P. *Listening to Learn: A Handbook for Parents with Hearing-Impaired Children.* Washington, DC: Alexander Graham Bell Association for the Deaf, 1990.

Altman, E. *Talk With Me! Giving the Gift of Language and Emotional Health to the Hearing-Impaired Child.* Washington, DC: Alexander Graham Bell Association for the Deaf, 1988.

Cohen, L. H. *Train Go Sorry: Inside a Deaf World.* New York: Vintage Books, 1995.

Featherstone, H. *A Difference in the Family.* New York: Basic Books, 1980.

Frederickson, J. *Life After Deaf: Impact of Deafness on a Family.* Silver Spring, MD: The National Association of the Deaf, 1984.

Greenberg, J. *In This Sign.* New York: An Owl Book; Holt, Rinehart and Winston, 1984.

Holcomb, R., Holcomb, S., and Holcomb, T. *Deaf Culture, Our Way.* San Diego: Dawn Sign Press, 1994.

Kisor, H. *What's That Pig Outdoors? A Memoir of Deafness.* New York: Hill and Wang, 1990.

Kushner, H. *When Bad Things Happen to Good People.* New York: Avon Books, 1981.

Luetke-Stahlman, B. *Language Issues in Deaf Education.* Hillsboro, OR: Butte Press, 1998.

Luterman, D.M., and Luterman, R. *When Your Child is Deaf: A Guide for Parents.* Parkton, MD: York Press Inc., 1991.

Mahshie, S.N. *Educating Deaf Children Bilingually.* Washington, DC: Gallaudet University Press, 1995.

Marschark, M. *Growing Up Deaf.* Oxford: Oxford University Press, 1996.

Ogden, P.W. *Chelsea: The Story of a Signal Dog.* Boston: Little, Brown, 1992.

_____ . *The Silent Garden.* Washington, DC: Gallaudet University Press, 1996.

Padden, C., and Humphries, T.L. *Deaf in America: Voices From a Culture.* Cambridge: Harvard University Press, 1988.

Patterson, G. *Living With Children: New Methods for Parents and Teachers.* Champagne, IL: Research Press Co., 1977.

Sacks, O. *Seeing Voices.* Berkeley, CA: University of California Press, 1989.

Schwartz, S., and Miller, J.E.H. *The Language of Toys: Teaching Communication Skills to Special-Needs Children—A Guide for Parents and Teachers.* Kensington, MD: Woodbine House, 1988.

Simmons-Martin, A.A., and Rossi, K.G. *Parents and Teachers: Partners in Language Development.*

Washington, DC: Alexander Graham Bell Association for the Deaf, 1990.

Simons, R. *After the Tears: Parents Talk About Raising a Child with a Disability.* New York: Harcourt Brace Jovanovich, Publishers, 1987.

Smith, P.M. *You Are Not Alone: For Parents When They Learn That Their Child Has a Handicap.* Washington, DC: National Information Center for Children and Youth with Handicaps, 1984.

Spradley, T.S., and Spradley, J.P. *Deaf Like Me.* Silver Spring, MD: National Association of the Deaf, 1985.

Stewart, D.A., and Luetke-Stahlman, B. *The Signing Family: What Every Parent Should Know About Sign Communication.* Washington, DC: Gallaudet University Press, 1998.

Tye-Murray, N. *Cochlear Implants and Children: A Handbook for Parents, Teachers and Speech and Hearing Professionals.* Washington, DC: Alexander Graham Bell Association for the Deaf, 1992.

Walker, L. A. *A Loss for Words.* New York: Harper and Row, 1986.

Zazove, P. *When the Phone Rings, My Bed Shakes: Memoirs of a Deaf Doctor.* Washington, DC: Gallaudet University Press, 1994.

RESOURCES FOR PARENTS

Organizations

The organizations listed here provide information and support for parents of deaf or hard-of-hearing children. Most were found through the joint efforts of professionals and parents and include both state and national organizations.

Alexander Graham Bell Association for the Deaf
3417 Volta Place, NW
Washington, DC 20007-2778
Telephone: 202-337-5220
(voice/TTY)
Fax: 202-337-8720

American Society for Deaf Children
2848 Arden Way, Suite 210
Sacramento, CA 95825-1373
Telephone: 916-482-0120
(voice/TTY)
Fax: 916-482-0121
Toll-free telephone:
800-942-ASDC (voice/TTY)

American Speech, Language, and Hearing Association
10801 Rockville Pike
Rockville, MD 20852-3279
Telephone: 301-897-5700
(voice)
TTY: 301-897-0157
Fax: 301-571-0457
Toll-free telephone:
800-638-8255 (voice/TTY)

Center for Research, Teaching and Learning
National Technical Institute for the Deaf (NTID)
Rochester Institute of Technology
52 Lomb Memorial Drive
Rochester, NY 14623-5604
Telephone: 716-475-6923 (voice/TTY)
Fax: 716-475-6580

Dawn Sign Press
6130 Nancy Ridge Drive
San Diego, CA 92121
Telephone: 619-625-0600 (voice/TTY)
Toll-free telephone: 800-549-5350 (voice/TTY)

Harris Communications
15159 Technology Drive
Eden Prairie, MN 55344
Toll-free telephone: 800-825-6758 (voice)
Toll-free TTY: 800-825-9187
Fax: 612-906-1099

National Association of the Deaf
814 Thayer Avenue
Silver Spring, MD 20910-4500
Telephone: 301-587-1788 (voice)
TTY: 301-587-1789
Fax: 301-587-1791

National Information Center on Deafness
Gallaudet University
800 Florida Avenue, NE
Washington, DC 20002-3695
Telephone: 202-651-5051 (voice)
TTY: 202-651-5052
Fax: 202-651-5054

Signing Exact English Center for the Advancement of Deaf Children
P.O. Box 1181
Los Alamitos, CA 90720
Telephone: 310-430-1467 (voice/TTY)
Fax: 310-795-6614

INDEX